IMAGINING

T0059467

IMAGINING

ALSO BY GARY BARWIN

Fiction

Big Red Baby

Doctor Weep and Other Strange Teeth

I, Dr Greenblatt, Orthodontist, 251–1457

The Mud Game
  (with Stuart Ross)

*Nothing the Same, Everything Haunted:
  The Ballad of Motl the Cowboy*

Yiddish for Pirates

For Children

Grandpa's Snowman

The Magic Mustache

The Racing Worm Brothers

Seeing Stars

Poetry

Ampers&thropocene

Bird Arsonist
  (with Tom Prime)

A Cemetery for Holes
  (with Tom Prime)

Cruelty to Fabulous Animals

*duck eats yeast, quacks, explodes;
  man loses eye*
  (with Lillian Nećakov)

The Fabulous Op
  (with Gregory Betts)

*For It Is a Pleasure and a Surprise
  to Breathe: New and Selected Poems*

*Franzlations:
  The Imaginary Kafka Parables*
  (with Hugh Thomas & Craig Conley)

*frogments from the frag pool:
  haiku after Basho*
  (with derek beaulieu)

Moon Baboon Canoe

The Most Charming Creatures

No TV for Woodpeckers

O: eleven songs for chorus SATB
  (with Dennis Bathory-Kitsz)

The Obvious Flap
  (with Gregory Betts)

Outside the Hat

The Porcupinity of the Stars

Portal
  (visual poems)

Raising Eyebrows

The Wild and Unfathomable Always

IMAGINING
IMAGINING

Essays on Language,
Identity & Infinity

by
Gary Barwin

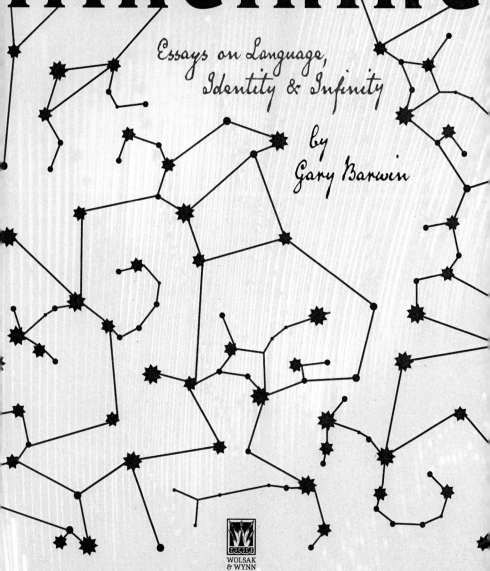

WOLSAK
& WYNN

Published by Wolsak and Wynn Publishers
280 James Street North
Hamilton, ON L8R2L3
www.wolsakandwynn.ca

Editor: Noelle Allen | Copy editor: AGA Wilmot
Cover and interior design: Kilby Smith-McGregor
Interior images: Gary Barwin
Author photograph: George Qua-Enoo
Typeset in Adobe Caslon Pro, Modesto Condensed and Old Man Eloquent
Printed by Brant Service Press Ltd., Brantford, Canada

Printed on certified 100% post-consumer Rolland Enviro Paper.

10 9 8 7 6 5 4 3 2 1

The publisher gratefully acknowledges the support of the Canada Council for the Arts and the Ontario Arts Council. We also acknowledge the financial support of the Government of Canada through the Canada Book Fund and the Government of Ontario through the Ontario Book Publishing Tax Credit and Ontario Creates.

Library and Archives Canada Cataloguing in Publication

Title: Imagining imagining : essays on language, identity & infinity / Gary Barwin.
Names: Barwin, Gary, author.
Description: Includes bibliographical references.
Identifiers: Canadiana 2023050258X | ISBN 9781989496794 (softcover)
Subjects: LCGFT: Essays.
Classification: LCC PS8553.A783 I43 2023 | DDC C814/.54—dc23

Contents

Broken Light: The Alefbeit and What's Missing *1*

The Ghost of Two Eyes *9*

John Coltrane Was My Bar Mitzvah Teacher *19*

Schrödinger's MS *29*

Wide Asleep: Night Thoughts on Insomnia *35*

Triaspora +1: The Sky on the Other Side of the World *43*

Elegy for a Poodle *53*

Other Happinesses: Magazines Are Good, Magazines Are Very Good *57*

Flying Is Just Falling with Good PR: On Writing *75*

Yes, and: The Ampersand, Twenty-Seventh Letter of the Alphabet *81*

Three Sides to Everything *85*

Meat and Bones *91*

Writing as Rhizome: Connecting Poetry and Fiction with Everything *97*

On Between *111*

That'll Leave a Mark *117*

The Archive of Theseus *125*

Sunshine Kvetches of a Little Parrot *131*

Language and a Half *141*

Hitler's Moustache, My Grandfather's Lip *143*

Racing Futurity *149*

Letter to You as if You Were Kafka *159*

The Selected Walks *165*

There's a Crack in Everything *175*

Endnotes *185*

Acknowledgements *187*

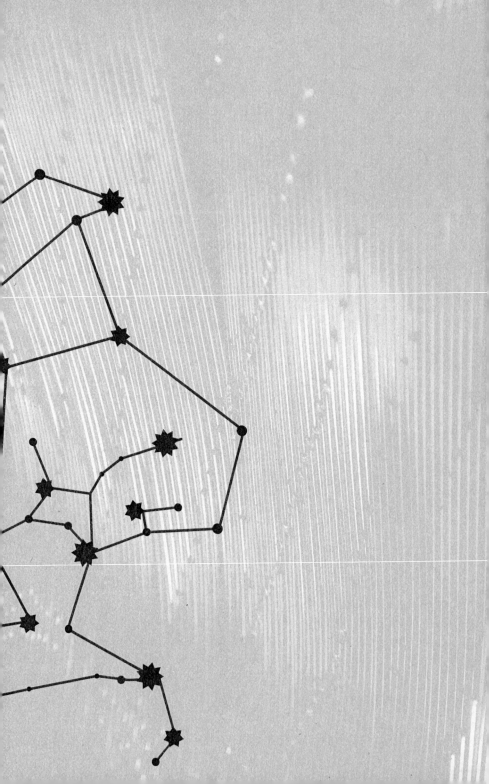

Broken Light:
The Alefbeit and What's Missing

When I was a little left-handed kid growing up in Ireland, we used fountain pens and I always smudged the letters as I wrote. I was really happy when I began going to Hebrew school and found out that Hebrew is read from right to left – the opposite of English. I could write clearly now while all the right-handed kids smudged their writing and got ink all over their hands. It was electric: this idea that language could be turned around. That it could make you look at things differently. Your inky hand. The page. Your way of being in the world.

In modern Israel, I know that Hebrew is used when asking for an oil change or when ordering socks online, but my first association with these particular letterforms, the Hebrew alphabet, the otiyot, was that it was the language of my ancestors. The shape of my people. Ancient, mysterious and numinous. Not that my ancestors didn't speak of socks and BO, but for centuries, Hebrew was a sacred language, not an every-day one. Its shapes: thick lines of black and white, each ending in a little curl like a black flame rising. Was this flame something to do with the temple? With eternal light? Or perhaps an arcane kabbalistic alchemy of words. The prayer books in the shul of my childhood were musty and worn, like the old tefillin of the praying men … or the threadbare carpets. The prayer books had been shaped by use, the way an old tool takes the form of the hand that touched it. It seemed like the Hebrew letters had also been shaped this way – they had been worn over millennia by the touch and speech of those who had muttered their sounds. And Hebrew, at least in the traditional shapes, seemed to preserve the motions of ink and brush, the motions of a scribe not writing so much as drawing the letters, his hand floating above the surface of the parchment like a hovering bird.

Rabbis and kabbalists look carefully at everything and make connections and draw inferences. Every element of the Torah can be examined as if it were made of atoms and molecules. And then looked at even more closely to reveal language electrons. Memory quarks and neutrinos. The Torah is a finite expression of the infinite, therefore this finite text can be examined infinitely. Little stories, little parables are told about the shapes and positions of the letters. For example, there is a tradition considering the fact that bet is the first letter of the Torah. It's like a square bracket at the very beginning of the text. It's closed on the top and bottom and on the right side, but it is open on the left. It means start here – it all starts here – and then keep going left in the direction of reading. Be open to what is to follow. The shape of the letter is an aphorism, a parable.

But it's not only traditional Jews who considered the shape of the letters and thought that they might represent something. According to the seventeenth-century Christian kabbalist and linguist, Francis van Helmont, Hebrew letters are "actually diagrams illustrating how the lips and tongue should be positioned when uttering the sounds they make." There has been this perennial idea that Hebrew letters have a unique connection to the physical world. For instance, in 1881, John Henry Broome wrote that the constellations which formed the zodiac could be shown to be derived from the Hebrew alphabet. The stars form Hebrew letters. And like the zodiac, it's often believed that there is an almost magic connection between the Hebrew letters and the world. For example, there is a tradition concerning the golem, a creature made out of clay. Some sources say that once the golem had been formed, one needed to write on the golem's forehead the Hebrew word for "truth" – "emet" (the letters aleph, mem and tav) – and the golem would come alive. Erase the first letter, aleph, and you are left with mem and tav, which is "met," the word for "death." Another way to bring a golem to life was to write God's name on parchment and stick it on the golem's arm or in its mouth. You would remove it to stop the golem.

This idea of concealing secret bits of paper, secret writings, in hidden places was full of mystery and intrigue to me as a child. Secret agents and pirates hid little scrolls in secret places. And it's true, like most Jewish families, even mostly non-practising ones like mine, we had a mezuzah on our front door. Inside the mezuzah, behind the letter shin, I knew that there was a little scroll with Hebrew letters written on it. They spelled out prayers, though I didn't know exactly what was hidden away on our doorframe. It made me think that there were aspects of the world that were ancient, that we couldn't see. There was literally more than meets the eye about our lives. What could that be? What was the story behind the story? There were superstrings and black energy, intimations of a network of invisible forces that were represented by these letters:

Tet	Chet	Zayin	Vav	Hey	Dalet	Gimel	Bet	Aleph

Samech	Nun	Nun	Mem	Mem	Lamed	Chaf	Kaf	Yod

Tav	Shin	Resh	Qof	Tzadik	Tzadik	Fey	Pey	Ayin

*

A few basics about the Hebrew alphabet, in case it's been a while since your Bar or Bat Mitzvah. Or since you last read *The Protocols of the Elders of Zion*. The Hebrew alphabet has twenty-two letters. None of them represents vowel sounds, at least not by themselves. Vowels are represented by little lines and dots and other symbols added to the letters. There are no upper- and lowercase letters in Hebrew, but there are a few letters that have special forms at the end of words. In Hebrew, some of the letters can be written with dots: the letters change sound if there is a dot in the middle. For example, the second letter in the alefbeit is called bet when it has a dot in the middle. Then it makes a *B* sound. When there isn't a dot, it's called vet and makes a *V* sound. The first letter of the Hebrew alphabet, aleph, is silent. According to Laurie Anderson lyrics – my authority on all things, though I think she's quoting tradition here – when you see an aleph you open your mouth to begin making a sound and then stop. Then you just think about the letter. The sound of aleph is all in the mind.

Like most written languages, Hebrew has different styles of writing and different typefaces or fonts. There's a very old one, which has the equivalent of serifs – that is, little decorations at the end of the letters' strokes, kind of like cowlicks. The other type of font is a more modern one. It is like a sans serif type and is much simpler – something like the Hebrew equivalent of Helvetica. Is there a Hebrew Comic Sans? There is a style of handwritten Hebrew, the equivalent to cursive, I suppose, which is different than the print form though the letters are also not joined together.

Though my interest in the elements of language comes from literature and experimental poetry, including visual poetry, my work is also influenced by Jewish mysticism, which, as I mentioned earlier, traditionally considers the shapes of Hebrew letters to be meaningful: elemental symbols inherently connected to creation and the universe. Edward Hoffman writes in *The Hebrew Alphabet: A Mystical Journey* that "the 13th-century mystical text, the Zohar, is filled with references to the importance of the Hebrew alphabet as a celestial code or blueprint for the cosmos ... Just as we now regard the DNA molecule as a carrier of incredibly condensed information concerning the development of life, so too have kabbalists viewed the Hebrew language ... as a cipher describing the universe." In this tradition, the letters are vessels made of the light of life itself, and recall the divine vessels that were broken at the time of creation. There's a story that says that when Moses smashed the stone tablets as he came down from Mount Sinai, the two tablets broke into a thousand Semitic smithereens, but the letters rose to heaven – even though they were carved into the stone. Another similar story tells of a rabbi being burned at the stake. His executioners wrapped him in a Torah scroll. As he was burning, he was asked what he saw. I don't know why they asked him this. Who knows what to say at such a moment? It's not like they make Hallmark my-condolences-on-getting-burned-at-the-stake cards to help out. But this rabbi answered them from the fire. He said that he could see that the Torah parchment was burning to ash but that the letters were ascending to heaven. I imagine it as a kind of alphabetic murmuration, a dark muttering cloud seeking infinity. But it is about communication: the idea of communication, and the promise of communication.

In the great Argentinian writer Jorge Luis Borges' famous short story "The Library of Babel" there are an infinite number of books in an infinitely large library. Each book contains some combination of only twenty-two letters. Borges, lover of all things kabbalist and writer of the stories "The Aleph" and "The Zohar," doesn't specify, but obviously he means the Hebrew alphabet with its twenty-two letters. Everything in the infinite universe, according to Borges can be represented by some permutation of the Hebrew alphabet – the foundational sacred alphabet, at least for the West. The twenty-two letters are the building blocks of everything. They are, in themselves, everything. Our world is language. Do we think in language, or do we only know what we think because of language? This recalls for me what it says in Genesis: the earth was without form and void until God gave shape or reality to it, all with words. With the letters that form the Hebrew alphabet. But are there things which cannot be represented in language? We know there are sounds that cannot be represented with our letters. We can only talk about these sounds. A fire crackling. A baby crying. The sound of a supernova. Maybe we hear a cow make the sound "moo" or a rooster say, "cock-a-doodle-doo," because the letters are a kind of lens, a window onto the world which only allows us to see a certain view, a certain quantity of light to reach our eyes, which themselves are a type of window. Just in case all my spritzing gives the impression that I think I'm a big macher who's knowledgeable about Hebrew, I should also add that, like many Jews who had a Bar or Bat Mitzvah, I learned how to read Hebrew, that is, how to recognize and sound out the letters. And then I learned how to chant using the little symbols added to the letters. But I never learned how to know the meaning of what I was reading (I did read the passage in English translation – it was something about King Uzziah and his throne). But not understanding Hebrew left me to think a lot about the shapes and sounds of the Hebrew alphabet, unimpeded by the distraction of knowing what the words actually meant.

There is a medieval kabbalistic text that says that there is one letter missing from the Hebrew alphabet. It will be revealed in the future. Every problem in our current universe is connected to this missing letter. An inconceivable letter that makes an inconceivable sound. We don't know what sound it might make. Its sound will make undreamed of words and worlds. Some think that this letter is the symbol that appears on the little black tefillin box that Orthodox Jews wear on their forehead for morning prayers. The symbol looks like the letter shin except with an extra arm, kind of like a *W* with an extra bit, a triple *U*. So, the thinking goes, we might already know what it looks like. But we don't know what new sound it might make, this new sound that might heal the universe.

I love this idea. That discovering a new letter might fix what is wrong with the world. That its new sound might heal the crack in everything. That we might discover that this new letter is already in the world, and we just need to know how to pronounce it. Or maybe that by playing with the shapes of existing letters, we might discover this mysterious missing letter and solve everything. This tradition imagines that the very letters of the alphabet are powerful. That they are magical. That the elements of our language – of our writing, of our speaking, of our communication – make the world, represent the world, speak back to the world, improve the world. That there is something to say that is just beyond our reach. For now. So of course I, too, believe this about letters. The idea that communication, the concept of language, the idea that language, speech and writing are themselves cause for wonder, curiosity and creativity. And, ultimately, because this undiscovered letter is there to be found, language is a cause for hope. But I would add that we also need to watch out for language's ability to lull us, to beguile us, to trick us with its deftness, its beauty, its ability to construct plausible and believable worlds, worlds which may misrepresent or ignore. We must always look very carefully at language. At its beauty, its mystery. Its power to make us think and feel things. Its power to make and re-make the world.

THE GHOST OF TWO EYES

They said my right eye was "lazy," as if there was something slothful, a bit decadent or maybe indulgent about that eye. Oh, they could fix it all right. If I didn't start using it more, they'd patch over the left, more achieving eye and make that right one work. Boyo. Later, it was determined that the back of my eye was not spherical like a marble but egg-shaped, like the dip in a spoon. It couldn't see properly, no matter how hard my brave little eye tried. It was astigmatic and everything was fuzzy. Even with glasses, they couldn't completely correct it. Unless, they said ominously, I lost my good eye, then measures could be taken. They never said which measures or why they couldn't just correct the eye now. And so I've never been able use binoculars or 3D glasses in the manner in which God intended. Or those antique stereoscopic things where two very slightly different images (the left-eye and right-eye view) of the same scene make the combined effect into a 3D scene.

*

I've just turned fifty-nine. LIX in Roman numerals, which perhaps better convey the one-less-than-sixtyish feeling that I have. I'm nearly there. About to turn a corner. Open a door. About to step over a precipice and hurtle ... where? I'm not sure. Into being older? Old. Is it to a place where I'm less worried, where I've arrived beyond some concerns I had throughout my younger days? I suppose I'm feeling that the end is in sight, even if I'm lucky and it is thirtysomething years away. In truth, I'm liking this life, where I'm at, what I can do, and I want more of it. I want it to continue.

*

I was thinking about the stereoscope because I misread a word in W.G. Sebald's *Austerlitz*, and in Sebaldian style, I realized how it was a good metaphor for the past. Or for memory. History. Our two views: how we saw something then, how we see it now. Or maybe, how our view of the present is affected by the past. We see the same image but from two different perspectives and it literally creates greater depth. This is either a good thing or a kind of illusion where we are tricked into thinking our view is closer to reality. Two different views blended as if they were one, and we lose the ability to see the two distinct components.

*

I'm beginning to think of the past – my past – with tenderness. Like it's an old dog. It waddles. Its eyes water. It leaks. I remember its leaps, its appetite, how it barked and protected us. The time it got away and worried us. The times it crapped on the floor. On the bed. I'm getting sentimental about even the bad things. At least they were *my* bad things. I'm lucky that nothing truly tragic or traumatic happened. Just loss, sadness, worry. A slow accumulation of troublesome experiences or knowledge, the ground slowly shifting rather than a sudden earthquake or tidal wave. I sense something like an accumulation of debris, sediment – fine sand with occasional sticks, stones, old tin cans – shifting around, forming dunes and undulations. It slows me down, but it is much less sharp than the rocks from which it was formed.

*

I never dated as an adult. My wife, Beth, and I first began seeing each other when I was eighteen and she was twenty. We never stopped. Or rather, we got married a few years after we met and here we are, forty years later. On one of our first few dates, we went on the rickety old Flyer roller coaster at the Canadian National Exhibition. It was the '80s and Beth was wearing a floofy sweater. I still had braces. I turned to say something just as the ride began, and I got my braces caught in the elaborate fabric of her shoulder. She thought I was just scared, but I was trying to extricate myself and my braces for the entirety of the ride as we went up and down and around.

Before we'd even spoken, Beth had had a dream where hundreds of people were being led somewhere and it wasn't good. We were in the line. It was an Irishy hill, grey sky, mist, a drystone wall. We picture it now as the Mourne Mountains. Dream-me led us away from the line and to a patch of brilliant sunshine. We sat on the wall in this bright warmth under a large and iconic tree. We were two people, coupled by our escape. A few years ago, when I went to Ireland, I bought her a tree necklace, which now she always wears.

Or she did. It got lost and so I had to buy her another identical one.

I visited a giant thousand-year-old bell in China some years ago. It looked in perfect shape, so I asked about it. It was a perfect replica. In China, I was told, they don't think of a recreation as any less authentic than the original. It carries its spirit.

The past is tricky. Sometimes we have to make it again. Ship of Theseus: solved.

*

Regrets? Yeah, I've had a few. Mostly, I'd like another chance at some things for which I was too anxious, or impetuous, or unprepared, so I could really appreciate them, enjoy them. But that's hindsight. Mine isn't even twenty-twenty with corrective lenses. Unless I lose my good eye, then I could be twenty. Just twenty. But you can only know what something was, what it will mean to you, after it was and not during. If there's too much "oh, this is something I'm going to remember forever," you aren't entirely in the moment. You'll only remember your advance memory of it. If I could only live through my circumcision again so I could really be in the moment. But you can't be too self-consciously in the moment. I think of the times when I would play squash and the ball would arrive in the perfect position for me to slam it with triumphant and stylish bravado. I'd be so aware that this was a perfect opportunity, a perfect moment, I'd flub the shot.

*

I wake up and think about the time my seven-year-old son somehow convinced me to cross a river barrelling through a steep gorge. The park ranger was shouting for us to stop. "But I've put my wallet in my shoe and thrown it across the river already," I said. We began to cross the river, lost our footing, swam like mad and made it to the far shore. We survived. We might not have. It was extremely dangerous, and I was the one in charge. But I've had this retrospective fear, this charge of "what was I thinking," so many times that it has lost much of its piercing terror.

*

When that same son was fifteen, our family was swimming at a Hawaiian beach. We'd hiked down a cliff to the remote beach because it had black sand and was open to nudists. The sand was amazing, but, much to our sons' disappointment, the naked people comprised only old hippies with sagging scrotums that looked like Hacky Sacks in long bags.

We went for a swim, but then the tide went out and the waves suddenly became huge. We were being tossed around, pulled from shore. Beth is a strong swimmer. She made it back to the beach, albeit deposited unceremoniously on her bum, her bathing suit filled with sand. I was struggling and unable to return to the beach, but then I felt strong arms around me, which lifted and swam me to shore. My son, recently qualified as a lifeguard. He'd rescued his little sister and then came back for me.

*

Some of the fears I've had over the years have gone underground and become part of what I am, part of who I am. Like toxins, my body has worked to process them, to integrate them, to neutralize them. I know they affect my thinking and behaviour. Some experiences never go away. They are ghosts inside you, haunting you. Whistling or howling, giving your gut chills.

*

When I first went for glasses, my father, a young man at the time, tried on several pairs himself. He found some that were just like his boss's, a more senior doctor. These are the ones you should get, Gary. And indeed I did get them. I once told a therapist this, and we thought it was telling: issues around the separation of father and child, the possibility of being who you really are, the expectation of parents and so on. Now, I see my father as young, with all the fears and worries of a young man trying to establish and prove himself in a serious career in a new country. Of course, he shouldn't have tried on the glasses himself and made me get them, but after fifty years, perhaps I'm ready to see this moment with compassion. And with distance. I've had plenty of chances to become who I am and who I want to be. My parents did provide me every opportunity in other ways. Maybe there is more to this memory, or perhaps it wasn't quite as I remember it.

It's entirely different than the time I tried on some jeans in a store in London, England, and the store clerk said, "Perhaps the young gentleman is too husky for these dungarees." Details like that you don't forget.

*

In Northern Ireland, during the Troubles, my mom used to campaign for the Alliance Party. It stood for what it sounded like – an alliance between the Catholic Republicans who wanted to return Northern Ireland to the rest of Ireland, and the Protestant Unionists who were in favour of continuing to be part of the UK. Our neighbour, Dr. Heel, an entomologist, made a huge *A* for Alliance on his front lawn by letting the grass grow long in an *A* shape, and cutting the rest short. He wanted the overflying British military helicopters to see. Another neighbour, Molly, used to call Roman Catholics "Rice Crispies," because of the initials R.C. And whenever anyone woke late, she'd say, "The dead have arisen and appeared to many," which is a line from the Gospel of Matthew describing an event after the resurrection. One time, my mom – who had a South African accent – while knocking on doors for the Alliance Party was asked, "How long have you lived here?" She explained, proudly, "Ten years." "Well," the Protestant woman said, "we've been here for three hundred. Come back when you've been here as long as us."

*

It's been one of my favourite lines of poetry since bpNichol quoted it in a second-year creative writing class of his that I took at York University.

> Goodbye as
> the eyes of a whale say goodbye, never having seen
> each other.

It's W.S. Merwin. I never thought of this line as sad until my friend Elee said so. Incidentally, a blue whale's eyes – and I do imagine a blue whale here – are surprisingly small for such a large creature. I wonder about these eyes: saying goodbye to each other, these grapefruit-sized eyes that have never gotten to know one another, living in two solitudes on either side of the massive head? I imagine the whale as having access to two mysterious and separate parallel worlds, the left and the right, tied together by the braid of its giant cetacean brain. The brain connects just like a stereoscopic image. Each eye relies on the other to explain its side of the world.

*

It couldn't have been later than Primary Four when I joined the entire Dunmurry Primary School to sit on the gym floor and listen to a bible story, told with the aid of a felt board and felt figures. A felt camel. Felt shepherds. A felt baby Jesus, a felt thirty-three-year-old Jesus. Mary and Joseph in flowing robes. A little felt manger. A felt Pontius Pilate. Was there a felt cross? Felt beads of blood and felt nails? I do remember the felt figure of Jesus being moved in procession, carrying his cross. And when they said, "The Jews killed Jesus," I looked around to catch my younger brother Kevin's eye. He was the only other Jew in the school, as far as I knew. What should we do? Be cool. Say nothing. And so I didn't.

*

> The eye you see is not an eye because you see it;
> it is an eye because it sees you. – Antonio Machado

Are there any creatures that can see their own eyes? Many have eyes on the opposite sides of their head, unlike others such as humans, which have both eyes pointing in the same direction but from slightly different horizontal positions for both depth perception and peripheral vision. Imagine Wayne Gretzky with eyes on the sides of his head like a whale. Now one of the great ones, skating between the waves, deking out the limitless sea. And then there are the horizontal slits of the pupils of goats, made, so I understand, to better see across the length of the horizon. Permanent landscape view instead of portrait.

*

This schoolyard carol parody from my childhood, when there were few television channels – only the government's BBC and the Independent Television network ITV:

> While shepherds washed their socks by night
> While watching ITV
> The angel of the Lord came down
> and switched to BBC.

Another schoolyard memory, this from the private school, Inchmarlo, that I eventually attended. A game where a boy wedged himself face forward in a corner while other boys lined up behind him. The goal was to push the first boy from his position and take his place. Each boy pushed on the one in front of him, trying to squeeze him out. The pressure on each other was enormous, especially those near the front – the combined force of all those boys, like a reverse tug-of-war.

*

We had little red hymn books, which fit perfectly into our black uniform jackets. If you were quick, you could pull out the hymn book, hit a boy on the head and return your hymn book to your pocket before a master saw you. I was never caught. Eventually, because I was Jewish, I asked to be excused from morning chapel, where the hymn books were used for singing. I was directed to wait in the dim boy-scented cloakroom among the coats, snacks (rock cakes!) and outdoor shoes. With me was a pale curly black-haired boy with a network of purple veins over his thighs. Julian. The only other Jew in the school. We became friends of a sort. I'd go over to his house to play chess.

*

I feel a bit bad, having told the story about my dad and the glasses. I was recently thinking of an incident around this time when we were in a restaurant airport and, across the room, a man in a wheelchair had turned bright red. He'd stopped breathing. If I recall correctly, he was choking. My father leapt up, ascertained the problem, unblocked the guy's throat so he could breathe again. I remember being amazed by my father's rapid dance of symptom-taking: airway, pulse, pupil dilation, lips, tongue swelling. I'm not sure what else he checked, but I was thrilled by the quick grace of my father, that as a young doctor he could rise from his sandwich and instantaneously switch into doctor mode, following emergency protocol to literally save this man's life.

*

In bpNichol's writing class, I doodled as I listened. One day I drew an image of two eyes. The left with a single pair of legs, the right with two pairs. The first eye held the other on a leash. A human eye leading a dog eye. I've begun to think of this image, over the years, as my logo. I like its tricky wink to hierarchy, as if one eye could be led by another, as if it could be a pet. What exactly is going on here? Is it a trompe l'oeil, a visual pun, or something from a folk tale? And here it is at the end of this essay as if it always belonged here, as if the metaphor of stereoscopic eyes on the past had already literally been embodied by me forty years ago. Is this the revisioning of history, something just to the left, just to the right of the truth, and yet somehow connected? Relational? The I of the present, the Thou of the past.

John Coltrane Was
My Bar Mitzvah Teacher

I began listening to the music of John Coltrane at the same time as I began studying for my Bar Mitzvah. As a twelve-year-old, I'd baby-sit Saturday nights for a variety of neighbours in my suburban Ottawa subdivision, and then on Monday I'd make an after-school pilgrimage to Sam the Record Man in the Bayshore Shopping Centre to spend my earnings on jazz records – not only Coltrane, but especially Coltrane. I'd return to my teak-shelved bedroom and devour the recordings, noting each detail of the accompanying text, design, photographs and music. On weekends, I'd go to the local public library with my grand-father and read all I could find about these musicians, their reeds and concerns, their saxophones and the sounds they pursued, the economic and political issues, the stories of their lives and of their mouthpieces. Of course, I had no real understanding of what it was to live their experience – my positionality was so different – but it was a portal, an opening that pointed to a much larger vision of what was and what was possible than I could otherwise have known.

When I went to synagogue and heard the chanting of the cantor, I heard echoes of Coltrane's free-form improvisations (for example, on "India," "My Favorite Things" or "Impressions"), and his exploration of modality and, particularly, the non-Western scales of Indian music. A solo voice keening, birling, undulating. I heard the expression of another kind of identity – what I imagined was an alternative to the four-square homophonics of the dominant Western culture. Homophony: when all the parts move together in lockstep, like European hymn singing.

In synagogue I heard something different. A kind of non-tempered heterophony – everyone singing their own version of the same thing, not quite together – or a monophonic – solo – swirling through different scales and otherness.

Sombre and plaintive, Coltrane's "Alabama" begins with the droning piano of McCoy Tyner, bells transposed down to dirge level and the plaintive cantillation of Coltrane's tenor, not weepy but a single voice in mourning. Then the tenor signals a key change, and the bass and drums enter and the track moves to a slow yet serious swing rhythm. They are moving forward, despite everything. It's life. And then silence. And the chanting saxophone returns to the plaintive opening melody, this time with soft mallets rumbling on low drums and the bass weaving sombre. This is retrospective – we're thinking back – yet there's been a gathering, a coming together, even in sadness. We don't forget; we memorialize, we honour. We speak as one.

In "Alabama," I heard the deep grief for Addie Mae Collins (fourteen), Cynthia Wesley (fourteen), Carole Robertson (fourteen) and Carol Denise McNair (eleven), four young girls murdered by the Ku Klux Klan in a Birmingham church. Coltrane standing with his tenor, expressing his sorrow and blessing them with this secular prayer. Sanctifying their experience. What felt like "our" experience, even though, I, of course, shared almost nothing of this experience, or Coltrane's, and came to it as a middle-class white Jewish teenager, fifteen years later in suburban Ottawa. But it revealed something about the world. This was what was important. This was how one responded with courage and a sense of empathy and morality.

It did make me consider my grandparents in Eastern Europe, the hateful system of apartheid that my parents left in South Africa, and the religious strife in Northern Ireland where I grew up. Later I'd think of it like Walter Benjamin's image of the angel of history being blown back into the future by the difficult past. "Where we perceive a chain of events, he sees one single catastrophe which keeps piling wreckage upon wreckage and hurls it in front of his feet" ("Theses on the Philosophy of History"). Yes, there's wreckage, but accumulating in front of the angel, there was also Coltrane and the work of other creators as they, too, were blown by catastrophe into the future.

Through "Alabama" and the model of John Coltrane, I understood that music and the arts in general could express profound feelings of empathy, a kind of large-picture view of the world, what might be termed "spirituality," as well as conveying its social or systemic context and the powerful senses of consolation, anger and healing through shared experience and expression. I understood, also, an energized sense of being-in-the-moment as it unfolds. The definitive version of "Alabama" appeared on the album *Live at Birdland*. I remember reading how it was remarkable that this profound and deeply moving piece was recorded live in a nightclub – Birdland – where people, out for a night's entertainment, were drinking their beers and cocktails.

On the Jewish High Holiday of Yom Kippur, when I went to synagogue with my parents, I heard the Kol Nidre prayer, which is one of the most serious, intense and emotional prayer songs in the tradition. I heard in it the sorrow of persecution and suffering of the Holocaust, and the suffering afflicted on other peoples at other times. Of course, because I was a teenager, I also heard a general cri de cœur for life's difficulties and fundamental existential dilemmas. But through this, I understood that such expression could bring meaning and perhaps consolation.

I also understood the model of Coltrane's relentless experimentation – his drive to discover and to explore what might be possible, rather than just continuing with the utter mastery that he had achieved. (For example, on *Kind of Blue*, that mind-blowingly perfect Miles Davis album, he joins Miles and Cannonball Adderley in creating solos of aptness and grace, each one already sounding like a classic as they unfold.) The role of the artist – and by extension, the role of the person – was to explore their art and to push through to greater understanding and expression. I saw those as two facets of the same thing.

In larger jazz groupings such as those of Charles Mingus, I heard another alternative to Western ideas of homogeneity, control and sleekness. I also heard this when I listened to recordings from traditional Black churches. They had a vibrant and, what often seemed to me, ecstatic combination of the individual and the group – heartfelt choral singing mixed with parishioners who were free to sing and call out, to embellish, to vary. Later, living in Windsor, I'd hear Sunday morning broadcasts from Detroit. Preachers performing a service that moved from spoken preaching to raspy and impassioned singing and shouting. A call from the preacher and a response from the bluesy organ and the increasingly emotional congregation.

I first encountered the opposite to this – Lutheran chorales, particularly those of Johann Sebastian Bach – while studying music harmony. A Bach chorale is a fortress: solid, impregnable, stable. Like most chorales they are in four parts so that small groups of Ilsas, Gretchens, Bernhardts and Fritzes could sing soprano, alto, tenor or bass. They are "harmonizations of a hymn or psalm sung to a traditional or composed melody in church," according to *Merriam-Webster*. These hymns are regular constructions, made of repeating sections of eight-measure phrases. They are a staple of standard music theory curriculum. I studied and sang many of them in my undergrad music classes not because there wasn't anything more thrilling than pretending to be a devout eighteenth-century European Protestant on Sundays in a Leipzig church, but because they demonstrate everything in miniature – voice leading and the principles of harmony and harmonization. I remember early morning classes when Professor Blum would point to me and tell me to sing from the chorale we were studying. Nervous, my already warbling baritone would falter. "That is woefully inadequate, Mr. Barwin," he'd say. In his class, we'd wait for the moment when he'd mix up his chalk with his ever-present cigarette and attempt to smoke it.

One of the most famous chorales is a setting of Martin Luther's "A Mighty Fortress Is Our God" ("Ein feste Burg ist unser Gott"). Like most chorales, "Fortress" has all of the singers moving in lock-step, sturdy beams of oaken quarter notes and eighth notes. Nothing immoderate or sensual. Beautiful and powerful music, but if you made a cabinet out of this chorale, it would be all right angles and would keep your serious black clothes safe in a storm.

I didn't go to services very often, but when I did, I went to a fairly old-fashioned synagogue. I loved those times where the cantor wasn't leading the service, instead the congregation of mostly older men would pray. Each man would mutter at his own rate, mumbling passages unintelligibly and then surfacing for a moment, speak recognizable words and chant, only to sink back below the surface of intelligibility again. As each man did this in his own way, the resulting texture was a complex weaving of voices, each individual part of an organic ever-changing community of voices. There was no regular rhythm and there were no chords: it was a braid of melodic simultaneities. Sure, I know now that these services of singing men were all part of a patriarchal and exclusionary tradition, but the musical texture was intriguing to me and was an alternative to the homogenous and lucid ideal of perfection of Western tradition, particularly that of the Enlightenment. Because it was irregular and did not seek perfection – no bel canto here, rather all sorts of idiosyncratic approaches to voice, rhythm, timbre, intona-tion, pacing, and an introspective expression for one's self and one's God only – it felt particularly imbued with a kind of mystic inscrutability and kabbalistic invocation of the numinous. It also seemed to be inter-twined with the body – old men sounded old, husky, wavering, innately imperfect and authentically their unvarnished yet farmisht selves. I felt that, like in services at Black churches and jazz ensembles, it embodied another tradition or way of thinking, of experiencing and being in the world that wasn't the dominant Western capitalism enlightenment that was all around me. A brilliant articulation and enaction of at least one kind of difference.

In the interests of full disclosure, I should address other music I encountered: I wasn't only a teenage Jewish jazzer, and though almost none of the music I was into was pop or rock – I did have a Rick Wakeman album and one by the Pretenders – it was other music that captured my imagination. Perhaps this complicates the previous discussion about finding myself through the lessons and inspiration of jazz and African-American culture, but I think that engaging with this other music is an alternative to the dominant capitalist MO of most of our culture. And in truth, many people find an expression of their otherness by inhabiting culture that might be implicated in other values. They're still able to discover themselves in it, for example, through irony, subtext or reclamation, whether from a feminist, queer or other lens.

I played recorder and cello avidly until I was about fourteen. I deeply connected with cello music – I remember requesting a boxed set of Pablo Casals playing the Bach solo cello suites for my birthday. The photo of Casals had a beautiful cinnamon-colour background, the hue of both the cello and its sound. Both cello and recorder were powerful voices for me, voices that I accessed through both playing and listening.

When I was eight or nine, my very favourite recording was Dvořák's *Cello Concerto*. I remember strongly tactile, or maybe more accurately synaesthetic feelings evoked by the cassette. The olive-yellow colour, the image of a thick yarn tapestry on the cassette cover, the metal blue of the label. The distant world of longing in the music. The sombre, intense and thoughtful clarinet, the larger heart of the cello in its role as deeply feeling protagonist. These were big emotions that I discovered in myself through listening. This was what it was to understand one's self, to have a "self" which could conceive of (and feel) emotional places outside of the everyday, yet places which affected how one saw one's daily life. The sun came in through the window. It was filtered through my experience of the cello's timbre. Walking in the woods had the tone of a recorder. The timbre of the trees, yes, but a vision of what medieval, Renaissance and baroque music knew about trees, how they felt about them then. Many things were in the Dorian mode, that scale from before Western classical music sorted itself into major and minor. I had Dorian feelings. Or Phrygian emotions.

I played lots of early music on recorder and then discovered Irish music (one reason for my interest was that it connected me with Ireland, where I had lived until I was nine). I had the Chieftains' *Bonaparte's Retreat* and a great The Boys of the Lough LP. I was listening for the usual tropes: bittersweet moments of melancholy, peat-infused tunes redolent of landscape, an engagement with myth and the ancient. T.S. Eliot wrote of "the objective correlative," by which he meant "a set of objects, a situation, a chain of events which shall be the formula of that *particular* emotion" ("Hamlet and His Problems"). I heard this music as if its elements were arranged to invoke these particular emotions, these particular relations with the world. There was the direct sensory pleasure of the music, but there was also this objective-correlative world-building through which I attempted to construct belonging, homeland and a sense of living in diaspora, replete with its particular and official emotions. I wasn't just living in suburban Ottawa. I was an exile.

And then I began saxophone in grade seven and my obsession with jazz.

This engagement with jazz would inspire me to ask questions about others. What was it like to be from Missouri? What was it like to seek, through music, to reinvent oneself? To search for a voice, a language, a way toward a larger narrative? To feel compelled to create and to explore new ways of creating? If you were Sidney Bechet, what did that vibrato say about your conception of life? There was that Gerry Mulligan duet with Dave Brubeck, "Sermon on the Mount," where I could feel my own teenage soul in the sound of his baritone saxophone, creeping, hollow, lamentatious, earnest, arboreal, prayerful.

Lester Young with the Kansas City Seven was the first LP that I bought. It was a sound from a time, a climate, an audioscape that was far from where I was, yet I felt it led me out of my green shag-carpeted bedroom, down the hot streets of a Kansas City night and into the perfect warm and spry choreography of its music.

I also remember going into the mall with a handful of Bar Mitzvah–acquired silver dollars to buy Moe Koffman's *Four Seasons*. It wasn't lost on me that he was a Jewish-Canadian jazz musician. The inside of Moe Koffman's double album had a photo of a bulletin board, ostensibly Moe's own. There were postcards, to-do lists ("buy bread and wine"), notes about recording, etc. This might be the kind of life someone who made the sort of music Koffman did could live. I could live it too. Maybe I was supposed to, one day, when I was an adult. Other kids around me had Ziggy Stardust and Iggy Pop to show them their own path, but I had this middle-aged Jewish Torontonian.

I don't remember what the rabbi taught me for my Bar Mitzvah. Ethical responsibility? Moral choices and culpability for one's actions? How Jewish text and musical culture could articulate values and identity, and form a way of being in the world? I remember almost nothing of that. I do remember him telling me that I should say "Moses's" instead of "Moses'," which rankled my Anglo-grammatical sensibilities – and I refused. I do think of the grief and consolation of "Alabama," of how Coltrane responded with compassion, empathy, moral courage, tenderness and strength. Coltrane taught me these valuable lessons – lessons vital to the project of becoming a Bar Mitzvah. He also enabled me to hear the music of my own Ashkenazi musical tradition.

I know that I am running the risk of essentializing both Black and Jewish experience, and I'm aware that it requires nuance and deftness to navigate these complex socio-cultural and appropriational issues. I am after all connecting my life as a middle-class Jewish kid from Ottawa to the imaginative, political, spiritual world of mostly Black American musicians. Of course, I didn't actually understand their experience, or, for that matter, the experience of those old men davening (praying) in the synagogue. It's rather that what they were doing was a way, a frame, through which I could understand my own experience, the way I organized my being in the world. These musics showed me another physics, they were another kind of Bar Mitzvah education.

So what does this mean? Why does it matter, this other education? Perhaps: The Jewish position is complex. White-ish. Until we're not. Not, until we seem to be. There are many alternatives to the dominant society. We can find allies in our struggle for understanding, our basic striving to be more deeply human. Jews, in addition to controlling the international banking system and following other protocols, have taken over Black music – you called it, Kanye. We've Al Jolsoned and Benny Goodmaned our way to power. Jews can also maintain their heritage of divergent thinking, our own epistemic and social traditions, even while being part of the larger society by finding support, parallels and inspiration in others' traditions as well as their own. Intersectionality includes us in its nuanced understanding of the complexities of identity. We all can find our own particular ways of expressing the world and finding expression in it. Not cultural hierarchies. Cultural webs.

Schrödinger's MS

or, the writing inside this box is the greatest/worst, I am therefore the greatest/worst. Everyone should love me/regard me with contempt.

I'm going to talk about something that isn't my favourite subject: my ego. I hope, though, that it's clear that what I'm talking about applies to most writers, perhaps in different ways, and we all have to manage feelings around both "success" and "failure" as writers and as people. And I hope also, as Whitman said, "All I mark as my own you shall offset it with your own, / Else it were time lost listening to me." To be honest, it's not that what I'm saying here is new, but it's something that I think isn't spoken about enough, especially among writers. And okay, maybe I am my favourite subject and just don't realize it. I mean, let's take a moment to think about my hair. Wow. Good. Now here goes:

I'm a goddamn genius! Love me! I just got the cover design and blurby words for my new novel. It's a really beautiful cover and the words are fantastic. They make the book sound amazing. And they said some tremendously complimentary things about me and my work.

This should be good, right? Of course it is. I mean, it's good for the book and for attracting unsuspecting readers. And I'm flattered and all. However, it makes me think about that oh so difficult of issues: What to do about positive feedback? It can make you uncomfortable. (Negative feedback is another thing – thanks, family! – but maybe what I say here about its opposite also applies.)

There is, of course, imposter syndrome. That couldn't really be me! What if everyone finds out that I'm a fake? I can't live up to those words. And for me, the book is done, so it's going to have to go out into the world without me. Nothing I can do will change the novel at this point. Unless, you know, I try to resume my affair with Vladimir Putin, accidentally discover a new planet or become a Kardashian. The novel is typeset and ready to go, and it's too late to fix that factual error someone found. But now that I'm working on a new novel, I feel haunted by the last ones. Can I make it as good? (The last ones are disappointments to me, of course – I wanted those books to be so much better – but also, can I make this novel as good as the last ones? It should be just like the last ones, except of course, totally different.) This is the quantum state, the Schrödinger's cat of self-regard that writers often live with. We're great while at the same time we're awful. Naturally, sometimes we're Mr./Ms./Mx. In-between.

Can any of my writing live up to the hyperbolic praise that appeared on my last book? It actually says, "a novel of sheer genius." What? But, of course, that's just advertising bumf. Sure, the editor thinks the book is good, but what does saying this kind of stuff really mean? It is the relationship between a reader and a book which determines how the book works. And that can be neither quantified nor predicted nor assumed. That's one of the things that's great about writing. It's always its own thing. And the reader makes it their own thing. Or not.

Of course, it isn't about the hoopla around the reception of the book, or how "great" I am or how terrible. I hope just to write. To make the book I'm writing be the best it can be. For the book. Sure, for my own satisfaction as a writer, also. I mean, I do take pride in my craft. If I were a wall builder, I'd want to make a good wall. But writing is different than building walls. There's the matter of "wisdom" or "greatness" or "super whizbang artiness that transcends mere artisan/craftspersonness," isn't there? What does that mean, though, for a writer? I mean, I do try to go for it. To try to put everything into what I'm writing. Not to be pretentious and gloop up the work by trying to be deep, but to really "bring it" when I sit down to write. Whatever that looks like at the time. Whatever that looks like for me. So, I do try to "go deep," but not to be deep for the sake of it, or performatively so. I try to hear right inside me, to think and feel deeply about whatever it is I'm working on.

Language, story, history, idea, surprise, image. And when I'm making a terrible joke, I try to really make it terrible to the best of my ability. And when I'm writing a character, I try to really make the portrayal "sing," whatever that looks like for the particular work.

I remember when my last novel received a surprising amount of attention, particularly after landing on the fancy-schmancy Scotiabank Giller Prize shortlist, I was quite depressed. Why? I guess I let it get to me. It was strange. Part of me always wanted that kind of approval and affirmation. It was all very glamorous and glitzy. But when I got it finally, I didn't like it. It seemed like it was saying that my worth as a person had to do with this success. And of course, that isn't the case. Sure, this was tremendously lovely recognition of something I'd worked hard on, and for my writing career in general, but it didn't – and it shouldn't – mean anything about me as a person. As a son, husband, father, sibling, friend, etc. As a human. But to be honest, it took me aback. If I acknowledged this award, it felt like I was saying that actually it did matter whether I achieved this recognition as a writer, it mattered as to whether I had worth as a person.

It took a while to sort this out. Why did I feel badly? I didn't want the recognition if it meant that I'd really wanted it. Needed it. Did the fact that I wrote strange books for thirty years before this, books that didn't get this mainstream recognition, mean anything about me as a person? Nope. Did this sudden mainstream recognition? Nope. It was good for the career aspect of my writing – book sales, some money, opportunities to write and participate in things, and it got me some teaching work. But other than that, my life is about me as a person. I like writing – even when I hate it – and I hope and try to keep getting better. And to have the opportunity to keep writing and to keep being able to share that writing in whatever form that takes.

Sometimes I worry when people speak to me about becoming "a

published writer" or about how putting out a book will change their lives. Sure, it will, AS A WRITER – maybe – but not as a human. We will still have the gaping holes of need inside us that we've always had, even if we have a #1 International Bestseller, six Nobel Prizes and a prize-winning cabbage. Or we'll still be filled with gladness and light if we don't. The only difference is, we'll have a publication, or a book. And that's a great thing. We get to write. And we get to be profoundly ourselves and work through all of what that means. But neither is dependent on the other. Writing gives us freedom and possibility, always. And we get to decide what matters to us, not what is important to the market, or to the prizes or anything else.

It's true that most of us have times when we get overwhelmed with insecurity, envy, doubt – the three sneaky codependent muses. And in some people, this leads not just to despair, despondency and depression, which are certainly bad enough, but to problematic behaviour, such as taking their feelings out on others, their poor behaviour fuelled by their own issues. What to do with the feelings? I mean besides becoming a radiant and self-actualized wonderperson. I've tried that. Apparently, it takes a lot of work, therapy and Gorilla Glue. For me, I try to take the negative energy and put it toward being supportive of other writers. Even if I haven't yet battled my own demons, at least I've done something good and helped someone. And of course, the poor feelings, the negative focus on myself is somewhat transmuted into something more positive. It also helps because it means I've stepped back and taken in a perspective larger than my own black hole of an ego.

Another thing is to understand that these feelings exist for many writers. Paul Quarrington said that envy, and the bitterness that results, "is the writer's black lung disease." So I try to be kind to myself, to think of that troubled writer-self as a child within that needs TLC (maybe THC sometimes, too) and nurturing. I'll protect tiny, worried little

Gary. Here, eat a cheesecake. Eat another. But really, I do try to take myself in stride and to channel the difficult energies into other things. Making art. Walking the dog. Being kind. Turns out these things aren't that hard to do.

Of course, I'm talking about garden-variety difficulties. Obviously sometimes things get way beyond that, and as unqualified as I am to talk about what I've been talking about perhaps too glibly here, I'm certainly not qualified to talk about the really heavy stuff. But I hear you. And myself at those times.

In the end, writing is in many ways as much about dealing with yourself as the writing. If only to get out of the way of it. But also, to work with yourself so that you can keep writing, to learn to navigate perceived successes and failures; to find renewable sources of creative energy and look after yourself despite or because of the challenges and rewards of your "career," regardless of what the jacket copy tells you.

WIDE ASLEEP:
NIGHT THOUGHTS ON INSOMNIA

For the past while, I haven't been sleeping, at least not properly, so my doctor ordered a sleep study. "How do I prepare?" I asked. "Practise," she said. When the time came, I went to the sleep lab and was ushered into what looked like a government office except with no windows and a bed that seemed intimidatingly functional. A young woman spent forty minutes sticking things to my body – wires to my head, to my potentially restless legs; two bands across my chest for my heart and lungs; a pulsometer to my index finger. The last time I had a sleep study, I woke in the night and began to read on my phone. The attendant rushed in, turned on the lights and exclaimed, "This is a sleep lab, now SLEEP!"

Did I sleep well this time? As Steven Wright says, "No, I made a few mistakes." If sleep were a story, there'd have been holes in the plot. Wormholes where I crossed into awakeness. Each time I awoke, I reached for my phone and read about the philosopher Baruch Spinoza. Take that, awakeness. I'll end you.

But instead, lying there under thin institutional blankets, I ended up not going back to sleep (at least not for a while). I was intrigued by what ol' Barry wrote, thought – oh, to be made cozy as if in a metaphysical onesie by Spinoza's notion that everything is because it is, that nature or God are the same thing as the universe, that the universe is a property of God or nature. As it says in the Stanford article on Spinoza, "Outside of Nature, there is nothing, and everything that exists is a part of Nature."[1] Inside, it's too dark to read.

I never believed in God per se, but I can "believe" in the universe because – expanding and made of inscrutable properties as it is – it exists. It means everything to me, because it is everything. I sweep my lordly hand in a literally all-encompassing gesture over not only our universe but all of them – multiverses then, now. Even the ghosts of future universes, gods (or nature) bless them every one. That everything.

Before I settled in for the night, I spent some time with a book I'd been reading about infinity – it's taking forever to finish – and, naturally enough, it talks about transfinities, the infinities beyond infinity. I love that one type of infinity is $\aleph_0$ – aleph-null[2] – a seductively kabbalistic Borgesian science-fictiony term. And that you can multiply infinity by infinity. Aleph-null by aleph-null and, like multiplying 1×1, you get what you started with. What happens if, when you're sleeping, you dream you are sleeping? This feels like another kind of infinity, another kind of sleep.

Sleep and infinity are related. Because you can never get enough of either? It's more that they both have the sense of venturing into a limitless space. What is the shape of the place that is sleep? It's edgeless, borderless, with no ground or sky. The composer Schoenberg imagined writing music that was like heaven – in this music, up, down, backwards and forwards would be the same because heaven had no direction and was thus entirely symmetrical. An angel has no upside-down, no matter how drunk it gets. I don't remember if Schoenberg spoke about time, but music that is symmetrical implicitly plays with time. If it is the same backwards and forwards, it doesn't operate in Newtonian time.

Knock knock.
Who's there?
Time traveller.
Time traveller who?
Knock Knock.

Except for the fact that I never get enough, sleep doesn't operate in regular time either. When we sleep, we slip out of time and into everything. Or at least, the possibility of everything. When it's dark, there could be anything in the room. Maybe you're not even in a room. Maybe you're everywhere. Of course the infinite bedchamber fills with one's finite worries: the ego, like a leash pulling a yapping dog running from yard to sidewalk, often snaps you back. The daily troubles, the nightly anxieties. Yeah, we can go skipping through the magnetic fields of the infinite once we've danced through the broken glass of psyche's parking lot. Did I just say that? Yes, I did. I must be dreaming if I think I can get away with such purple prose. But while we're here, thinking of the colour of sleep, of the psyche, of night, I'm reminded of poet Christopher Dewdney's remarkable phrase, "stars drip out of the cutaneous erectile velvet blue bandshell night."

Before we continue, a word about digression and association. Association seems apropos to sleep (the original Rorschach test) – borderless irrational night, ten-dimensional dream, time as an infinitely sided crystal made of pure possibility and quantum entanglement. Almost anything can relate to sleep. The endless monkey bars of darkness. The chocolate bar wrapper of night. Ten emus lined up, shaggy, ready to brush against your closed eyes.

Night is day's bruise, where light gathers beneath the surface like blood having burst from its vessels. (And back to concepts of God: the kabbalists speak of "the shattering of the vessels," which contained divine light. Sparks, like glitter, got everywhere. It's humanity's job to repair the world – tikkun olam – by collecting all this divine light.) Sleeping can feel like that – our task is to gather the dark sparks of sleep to heal the day, ourselves, the world. It's a time to line up emus.

I said that sleep seems borderless. Outside of a dog, sleep is man's best friend. Inside of sleep, it's too dark to see the borders. It's a joke that doesn't quite land, and let's not get diverted by how dogs and night and sleep are related, or even how dogs, the underworld, death, darkness and sleep are connected, though one of them is infinitely more slobbery than the others. The sleep state can spill – like the sloshing of an overfull psychological bathtub – into day. I'm not just talking about the daily need to be defibrillated by coffee, but rather the sense of processes begun in the night, the continued chthonic churning. The boundary-ness of the mind. You spent the night "sinking, sinking sleeper," as "the dark pines of your mind dip deeper,"[3] to quote Gwendolyn MacEwen. And now that you've woken, you're aware that the elemental world is there, below the surface, the underwater trees reflected in the aboveground forest. Some days, deep into the day, I feel this presence, expanding and informing my range of reference beyond the stumpiness of my usual diurnal concerns.

I have some small intimation of possibility, of the vastness of, well, everything. The interconnectedness of it all. I can't possibly imagine infinity or even a measly light year, but I can imagine imagining them. I can conceive of conceiving of them. I know that the universe is vast beyond reckoning. As Douglas Adams says in *The Hitchhiker's Guide to the Galaxy*, it's "big. Really big. You just won't believe how vastly hugely mindbogglingly big it is. I mean you may think it's a long way down the road to the chemist, but that's just peanuts to space."

I know I shouldn't make the mistake of imagining that the limits of my imagination are the boundaries of existence. I mean, twenty-two dimensions? Who could imagine that? Physicists got there through math. They proved it was so and so, they had to get their heads around the concept. At least to imagine imagining it. I think this happens with artists, too. The work leads them to burn "for the ancient heavenly connection to the starry dynamo in the machinery of night" (as Ginsberg writes).[4] But what is the actual world and what is our projection of it?

Unless the whole thing is a simulation and we're being simulated. As the old parable goes:

> Zhuang Zhou was a philosopher in ancient China who went to sleep one night and dreamt that he was God. "Wow, I'm the kind of philosopher who'd be great to date – I think of everything!" he thought to himself in his dream. When he woke, he didn't know if he was God dreaming he was Zhuang Zhou or Zhuang Zhou dreaming he was God. Then he went onto an ancient Chinese dating app, and discovered that he actually was Zhuang Zhou. "At least God doesn't think He's Zhuang Zhou," many of the prospective dates said.[5]

But I wonder, if you were Zhuang Zhou dreaming you were Zhuang Zhou and then woke up, would you know if you were the awake Zhuang Zhou dreaming you were Zhuang Zhou, or the sleeping Zhuang Zhou dreaming of the awake one? Guess you'd have to pee to find out for sure. But truly, I don't always know if I'm me dreaming I'm me, or at least the dream version of me, or if I'm actually entirely different – some other me dreaming that I'm me. Except I wake up through the night ("Did you sleep well?" "Only while I was sleeping.") and find myself there, in my onesie, Zhuang Zhou, not a butterfly, not even Groucho Marx, but hypnagogic me in a dark room, lying in my bed, my body the boundary between night and me. Between sleep and me. Between me and everything else.

Do you know the old Sufi fable about a yokel who goes to the big city? Afraid that he'll forget who he is, he ties a string to his toe, so he'll always know. When night falls, he goes to sleep in an alley. A wag plays a trick on him and switches the string onto his own toe. Upon waking and seeing the string tied around the other's toe, the yokel exclaims, "If you are me, who then, in God's name, am I?"[6]

I immediately have the impulse to imagine the story from the POV of the string. Tied around one toe or another, the string is still string. The sleeping string. The string awake.

"Whoa," the string says, echoing my thoughts, "I have consciousness and language. Also, an intuition of other parts of self. Mind/body is a kind of Gordian knot. A Möbius strip. Also, I'm kinda worn out."

"Aren't you just a piece of string?"

"I'm a frayed knot."

What I'm saying is quite obvious, a bit like one of those poems that say, "Wow! Daffodils. They sure are one of the things that we encounter in life," or "OMG, an escalator! It's like the stairs are climbing you," or even "I feel like I'm cheating on this sleep study because the guy in the room next door is snoring loudly enough for both of us."

It's a variety of noticing, of celebration. Of valuing.

What did I learn from the sleep study? Don't sleep beside a guy who snores. Also, don't sleep on my back. I stop breathing one hundred times an hour if I do.

Also, night is the other day. Sleep in all its wake-dappled uncertainty uses my brain as a telescope dish to collect everything it can – communication from the edges of things, the fossil glow, light from the deep past. It gives part of me access to myself when I'm not watching – except when I am. All those things I wished when blowing out candles, those thoughts I had on New Year's Days. Those undertows that pulled me out to the deep where there were sharks, mermaids, dolphins or my daddy. It gives me new possibilities. Sleep like a butterfly, wake like an ancient Chinese philosopher.

Like Penelope, sleep weaves everything together and then unweaves it.

The sleep doctor was clear. Like Theodore Roethke, I wake to sleep and take my waking slow. But I also sleep to wake, often repeatedly.

Midway through night's journey, the straightforward path is lost. And so? I've decided that it means I get to be aware of sleep many times a night. Of finding myself. Of drifting into consciousness. Of drifting out of it. I'm trying to learn what I can. Sleep isn't just so we can charge our phones and ourselves.

We say "deep sleep" and "wide awake." As if sleep meant being buried and awake was an open door. But really sleep, even when interrupted, is also wide. A wide-open space, though often dark. Wide as sky or deep ocean. As a yawn. As dark itself. Wide asleep.

TRIASPORA +1: THE SKY ON THE OTHER SIDE OF THE WORLD

1.

Six hundred and forty thousand one-hundred-year-old brass fasteners were removed from soldiers' paper records that were digitized and then destroyed by Library and Archives Canada. What to do with them? Artist Sarah Hatton used these brass "brads" to replicate the stars that would have been seen the day after Vimy Ridge, Ypres 1915, the Somme, Passchendaele and Ypres 1918, five of the bloodiest Canadian battles of WWI. These were the stars in the night sky that surviving soldiers would have seen from those battlefields in France. I can't help thinking, they were also the constellations that kept watch over the dead.

I look out my window at the sky, at the largeness of everything – there's so much more beyond what's visible, no matter how much I try to Hubble my eyes – and I wonder how, of all the places in the world, I ended up here in Hamilton, Ontario. It's been a good place to spend the last thirty-three years, but you might be surprised to know, it isn't included in Jean Cocteau's list of the three most magical cities in the world: Seville, Peking [*sic*] and Venice.

My family lives in exile. Supposedly. According to mainstream Judaism, we've lived in exile for nearly two thousand years. In exile from where? Israel, ostensibly. Almost on the other side of the world. The traditional once-and-future homeland of the Jews. Though we could easily move there now since the State of Israel was created in 1948 with nary a moment of complication or strife from the equanimous wreckage of various empires including the British and the Ottoman. The Israeli government recognizes the "law of return," which means that all Jews have the implicit right to move "back" there. Going to Israel is known as "making Aliyah." Ascending to Israel. Returning home. I could do it. If I wanted to.

We'll discuss Israel, Zionism and what is considered by many to be the proper home for the Jews in due course. In my novel *Nothing the Same, Everything Haunted*, my protagonist has a horse called Theodor Herzl, which won't go where it is told but keeps wandering off in the direction of Israel. And here I am, thinking back not to "the Promised Land" but to what has been for centuries "the compromised land"; to Ashkenaz, the thousand-and-something-year home where Eastern European Jews wandered. Ashkenazi Jews. And in my case, Lithuanian Jews. Litvaks.

Sometime after midnight, I walk to the middle of nearby Churchill Park. I look down and see right through the earth, to the stars on the other side. I see what those antipodean people sticking out in the opposite direction can see, gazing into their portion of sky. It's because of an app for identifying stars. Of course, it's always an app. Usually, I hold my phone up to the sky and it draws connections between stars and tells me the constellations, distance and star size. Every stelliferous thing my non-starry heart wants to know. But when I point my phone at the ground, the app tells me what is in the sky on the other side. If I dug a tunnel to China, as we tried to do as children, I'd know what stars would be at the end of the tunnel, even during the day.

My family has lived in the diaspora. The not-Israel. The not (or non-) home. We're not indigenous. We're ectogenous. Yet always aligning ourselves with our storied homeland. Our synagogues point toward Jerusalem. If we were pigeons, it'd be where we'd fly home. If we were IDF jets, we'd go there, too. At Passover, when the Seder Haggadah has Jews say, "Next year in Jerusalem," I've always wondered, "Really? Next year, I'll be here (wherever that is)." What connection do I have, a modern secular Jew living in Canada, to a place thousands of miles south of where I've lived, its palms and camels, ancient sand-coloured buildings, ruins and governments that make Pontius Pilate look good? I mean, sure, history. It'd be fascinating, but I've committed to here, to where I live, to our life here, our trees and social policy, to acknowledging our colonial history. I've committed to our hopes of making things better. Rivers, snow, Stan Rogers and Snotty Nose Rez Kids. I want to live in the present, not the past, and I don't want to live in a place purpose-built for one people. Despite the Holocaust. Despite anti-Semitism. Maybe because of it. I hope for equality and equity for all people here. And to keep working for a society that values it. That makes it happen.

I was born in Northern Ireland, the son of two South Africans, themselves the children of Jewish Lithuanian immigrants. My family kept moving through the twentieth century in search of work and security, and for a place to avoid persecution and political unrest. Each generation immigrated to and had children on a different continent. Europe. Africa. North America. I think the pattern might have stopped with my siblings' and my children. So far, all of them adults, they have continued to live in Canada. I have many complicated feelings (don't we all) and associations about the places my family was really "from." Where our home apparently is. Was.

Diaspora, from Greek. The term originated in the *Septuagint* (Deuteronomy 28:25), the Greek translation of the Hebrew Torah. The text is already a kind of migration – a translation, which itself means "carried across" – the Hebrew living in diaspora.

2.

DIASPORA[1]

My maternal grandfather was called Percy Zelikow. Back in Lithuania, he was Pesach Zelikowitz. My mother jokes that he was a self-made man who loved his creator. He used to say that the town he came from was so small that if you began to say its name as you walked in, you'd have walked out of it before you'd finished. How small was it? Let me say it. *Krakenova.* I think I got to the blacksmith shop by the second syllable. *Krakenova.* It was a shtetl in Lithuania, near the big city of Kaunas. In the late 1920s when my grandfather emigrated, that big city wasn't that big. The mayor's car had the number 1 as a licence plate. There were only nine other cars.

Like the rest of my family who escaped the Holocaust, my grandfather immigrated to South Africa, though before the war. It was a place Jews were allowed to go. I mean, other than Siberia, where his entire shtetl was sent during World War I. And then the shtetl was burned down. South Africa had opened up due to gold and diamond mining, and there was a need for the kind of middleman merchant jobs Jews could do. I think of those who left before the old country got too bad – the point where they'd actually be killed – as "prefugees." A few years later and they'd be hiding in ditches and trying to cross borders at night, hidden under bags of potatoes, if escape was even possible.

Of course, my grandparents' Lithuanian neighbours never really liked Jews, despite how the community flourished there. Vilnius had one hundred synagogues and was known as the Jerusalem of the North. But there were countless pogroms and persecutions. During the First World War, the Czar believed that the Jews were communicating with the Germans by hiding telephones in their beards. Really.

Diaspora[1], the world of my grandparents' youth: the old-world Jewishness I imagined. Yiddish and salted fish. Bagels and kugel. Samovars and silver candlesticks. My great-grandfather the blacksmith.

My grandparents never spoke of Lithuania – almost the entirety of their family who couldn't leave had been killed in the Holocaust. I think of this as "not-stalgia," because some places you don't want to look back on, recreate and live in the pain – the opposite of the fond if bittersweet tenderness of nostalgia. Despite this, my grandfather Percy spent his life looking for family he'd been separated from. I've written elsewhere about how he found his nephew Isaak in Chicago. I dedicated my novel about the Holocaust to Isaak who escaped Lithuania as a small boy by literally walking out of the country.

I feel a kind of heritage, of belonging to that pre-war old-world culture, and it wasn't just because of *Fiddler on the Roof* and Isaac Bashevis Singer. Perhaps it was nostalgia by proxy, once removed. My father in particular was charmed by the coherent iconicity of that world imbibed from his father and so, perhaps I felt a Jewish saudade for his sense of that lost world, which he had never seen directly.

Dia – across; *speirein* – scatter, disperse. But *speirein* is also to sow, and *spora* – seed. Diaspora: a handful of seeds scattered across lands. Sown. In my family's case, scattered once, twice, three, four times. Translated over oceans. So what is the word for having more than one diaspora? I imagine *dia*, instead of originating from "across," coming from *di* or *dis*: twice. And therefore triaspora. Quadaspora. Quintaspora. And on to endless-spora.

DIASPORA^2

Because my grandparents left Lithuania in the early thirties, my parents were born in South Africa and grew up during apartheid. That's like saying, "They grew up when people didn't believe in gravity. Or other people." Like everyone with darker skin, my father had to carry a pass to identify his race, though his card said, "white."

Diaspora^2, South Africa and my parents' memories and nostalgia: everything from the Barwin hotel, owned for a time by my grandfather, to boerewors sausage, game reserves and images of the Drakensberg (mountains) and all the African art in my parents' and grandparents' houses. I saw the art as evocative of this place they once lived, this place they spoke of with fondness and nostalgia. It was, of course, in part, also colonialist appropriation. When I was a small kid, I remember the one time we travelled to South Africa to visit family and seeing "the boy" who lived in an unadorned concrete room at the back of my dad's parents' garage with his unpainted bicycle. He was so thin, his hair so short; he was so young. I didn't know what to make of it, and so I didn't make anything of it. Except I didn't forget.

In 1960, the Sharpeville massacre marked the beginning of real civil unrest and violence. White police killed sixty-nine unarmed Black protesters. All too familiar. Of course, my twentyish parents were privileged whites, but they still couldn't abide this immoral regime. And it was becoming too dangerous. So they got married, my father got himself accepted to medical school in Northern Ireland and they moved. And that's how I was born in Ireland in 1964.

The psychogeographers write that place haunts us. And place is itself haunted. Saturated by life. By memory. Battlefields soaked in blood. Barns with milk. Secret places with tears. Sweat. My novel *Nothing the Same, Everything Haunted* says this explicitly. Nothing is the same as it once was, as it ever was, as it will be. It is haunted by its story, by our stories, by our memories of story.

DIASPORA[3]

Northern Ireland in the '60s and '70s was a remarkably beautiful if parochial place. Much of it really does look like a postcard of itself. The vibrant green of the Glens of Antrim. The craggy drama of the Atlantic coastline. The gloaming melancholy of the Mourne Mountains where we had a whitewashed cottage.

And then "the Troubles" began – the civil war between the Republican Catholics and the Unionist Protestants. Political turmoil seems to follow my family like feathers follow a duck.

I remember my father telling me the one where Hymie Goldberg is driving home when he's stopped by a masked man with a gun. "Are you Catholic or Protestant?" the man demands. "Ha! I'm Jewish," Hymie replies. "Sure," the man says, "but are you a Catholic Jew or a Protestant Jew?"

I look up. The sky is the birthright of all earthlings. But I don't really know the names or positions of the constellations beyond the few obvious ones: Big Dipper. Orion. Cassiopeia. From my position here in the city, in the first quarter of the twenty-first century, I feel that I live somewhat in diaspora to the stars. My ancestors once knew the sky and the natural world intimately. Now I mostly know them from books and media. When I've travelled, I've seen the sky crammed with light, stars pressing down on me in twinkling flocks. Mostly, all I see are the few that are visible in the densely inhabited places where I live. The stars are "mine," because I live on Earth – or for that matter in the solar system – but I feel in exile from them. I am far away from them not only in terms of distance but also in terms of knowledge and how much they are part of my "daily" life.

As a child I was insulated from sectarian violence. We were middle class and lived on Edenvale Park in Dunmurry, a village in the suburbs of Belfast where both Catholics and Protestants lived. Though one time a British soldier at the end of our street let me hold his machine gun. What was he doing at the end of our street? What was he doing letting me hold the gun? "Acka-acka-acka," I went. Not sure who or what I thought I was shooting at, but there was the imagined pleasure of doing it. We also used to play chicken with helicopters near an army base. Going close to it and then running like hell into the bushes. Sometimes neighbours had their downtown businesses bombed. My parents decided to leave Ireland when there was a bomb scare at my brothers' school, which already had barbed wire on the roof. Never mind a glass ceiling.

DIASPORA[4]

We immigrated to Canada. To Ottawa. I admit I did get worried when I went to university in Montreal at the beginning of the '80s and there was an acute rise in separatist sentiment, but I felt that, finally, my family had found a safe place to live. My wife, Beth – originally from Hamilton – and I moved to Hamilton about thirty-three years ago. Beth, a criminal lawyer, found her first job here. So yes, we moved to Hamilton for the crime. Our three children were born here.

I know that many Jews solve the problem of home by imagining Israel as the place where they originate from and where they belong. Gey gezunterheyt. Go in good health. Whatever Israel is, it doesn't feel like home to me. And some want to find their place in some heritage from the old world. But it doesn't and never did exist in the way they imagine it except as an ideal or as a story. And what did exist changed because of time and history. The old world was changed by the twentieth and twenty-first centuries. By the Holocaust. By Communism. When I think of what my brain is like inside, perhaps you won't be surprised to know that I think of fog. Fog rolling through the brooding, beautiful, narrative Mourne Mountains.

Are these multiple other space-times my heritage? I don't know the language(s), the customs. Maybe I could imagine one of my ancestors sticking their entire arm into brine and searching for pickles in a barrel, picnicking on Table Mountain, eating an Ulster fry at the pub. But even if these things were true, viewed from well into the twenty-first century, they seem entirely different now. Like Pierre Menard in the Borges story writing authentically as if he were Cervantes. But though he sounded exactly like the master from La Mancha, it wasn't the same thing at all. Menard being a Frenchman writing centuries later in this antique Spanish, and writing in a world that already had a Quixote. Maybe that's the most quixotic part about the project.

There's an old Yiddish saying, "The tongue is not in exile." It means that if you have to leave your home, even if you have to leave everything behind, even if you bring nothing but the clothes on your back, you always bring your language with you. Your words, your sayings, your stories, your jokes, your sounds, your culture, your world view. Even the ways you move when you speak. When I think about Yiddish, I move my shoulders in a certain way. I know I'm pantomiming and exaggerating, but it makes it legible to me. The world has a certain texture, a certain philosophy, a certain physics, and it's carried in the language. Yiddish is a library of our experiences, and it has travelled with us through time and space. But I don't speak Yiddish. I don't have those customs. They have faded like a tablecloth brought from the old country, washed a thousand thousand times until it disintegrated. I wonder: If not for the Holocaust, would I speak Yiddish?

It feels like a line has been cut. From my ancestors to me, history's severing of cultural transmission, the necessity of creating new diasporas. More and more I believe that this is what my culture is: a cut. I want to see it like the separated axon and dendrite of synapses, bridgeable by a leap. A translation. And a translation of a translation.

In quantum entanglement, two particles relate over great distance without any detectable connection. Somehow, though, they know. This is how I am entangled in these polyphonic histories. Transmission is a complicated tangle – a messy weave – of broken threads, which includes new threads acquired along the way.

Where is home? In language, culture, family, body? A stew – a tzimmes, a goulash, a jambalaya, a salmagundi – of my cultural triangulations. I've never lived in South Africa, yet I feel a nostalgia by proxy. I've never lived in Lithuania. Yet again, I feel proxy memories informed by what I've read. What I've learned, remembered, half remembered. What hasn't been forgotten. What I claim or wish to claim.

What my parents, grandparents and my children long for. Or what they don't long for. My inherited or future nostalgias. Not-stalgias. Maybe the places where my children might move in the future might one day feel like another kind of diaspora to me. Am I feeling pre-diasporic?

What's the difference between living in multiple diasporas and a family's history? About two pounds. Do these diasporas feel like where you're "from"? Where you were made? (The diaspora of your parents' bed?) The place, the culture. You miss it. This part of your identity, it feels like part of your DNA in all its contingent complexity. Its deep grammar informs your life.

My daughter, born in Canada, just discovered that due to a variety of citizenship laws, she is eligible for five different countries' passports: Canada, Ireland, the UK, Lithuania and Israel. It's the same for me, except that I could have one more: South Africa. There's paperwork to go along with my grammar of connection to these countries.

What to make about identification with these places where my family has lived? Across the ocean, through the ground, into the past. What stars were in the sky above Krakenova when my grandfather was a boy – the same remote light from the same stars as those Canadian soldiers in France – or later, above the house in Panevėžys, where my father's grandparents were killed by Nazis? What did they see, looking out of their windows that night? Could I know the sky above the hospital where my mother was born? These constellations from now, from memory and from the memory of others' memories. These stars on vaulted ceiling of my skull. Witnessing..

Elegy for a Poodle

All through the week, our old dog, Pepper, became more and more ill with the lymphoma that had been diagnosed a month before. By mid-week she was gasping for breath and her heart was beating frantically. At about 2:00 a.m. on Thursday morning, my wife, Beth, and I made the decision to go to the emergency clinic to have Pepper put to sleep. We woke our teenage sons: Aaron, the younger one, wanted to come with us. Ryan, our eldest, preferred to stay home with his nine-year-old sister, Rudi, who we'd let sleep. We thought she'd be too upset.

Pepper was my old friend, and I felt sad. At the same time, I thought of all the humans I knew who had suffered and were suffering, and felt lucky that it was the dog and not my wife or children who had become ill. I didn't cry until Aaron started to cry, holding the dog and whispering to her, consoling her as the vet found a vein and then stuck the needle in.

We carried Pepper home in a large coffin-like cardboard box that the clinic provided and stowed her downstairs until we could bury her in the backyard. In the morning, Rudi asked why Pepper had had to die in the night without her. "I should have been there. I could have helped her not to be so scared."

The next day it rained until suppertime. Then Ryan and I went out back with a shovel and dug a hole. Afterwards, Aaron and Rudi went out to enlarge the hole. They wanted to make sure that everything was exactly right.

Before we took Pepper outside, Beth opened the box to let Rudi see Pepper for the last time. Together, they spoke to her and patted her. They told her how they would miss her. That they loved her. They told her what a good dog she had been.

When I am dying, it would be comforting to be told that I had been the human equivalent of a good dog. Loving, compassionate, faithful, understanding, dignified, but also goofy, curious, fun, protective, a friend. Let's leave out obedience. Pepper never placed much value on obedience. She was more like a cat, winding her life around the family based on her own priorities and concerns – which, happily, included each of us.

We carried Pepper out to the hole and lowered her in. Then – as is done in Jewish burials – we took turns placing spadefuls of earth on top of her. There is that sound of the earth falling on top of the coffin, or in this case, the dog.

All that day, I wanted to write a poem for the funeral, something that would speak for us and make sacred this scene: my family gathered around the grave of this sort-of member of the family. At the same time, the impulse to write a poem and to invoke pet-loss solemnity seemed ridiculous.

I had written a funeral poem for a pet only once before, when Aaron was five and dealing with the loss of his goldfish. "Dad, you're a writer. And you play music. Please do something," he pleaded. So I wrote a poem – a blessing, really – for his fish, Sharky. Then we all stood in the backyard while I read the poem and played something elegiac on, of all things, a baritone saxophone.

Soon after, my grandfather died and we gathered again in nearly the same spot to plant a fruit tree in his memory. We told the kids that the tree would grow "grandpa peaches" for years to come. My grandfather was always amazed that he'd lived long enough to have great-grand-children. And he marvelled at that idea, that since he'd known his own grandfather, he'd therefore known six generations of his family, on three continents, with birthdates spanning 150 years.

In the Jewish tradition, mourners gather at the grave a year after the funeral and "unveil" the headstone. Until then, the grave has no stone. At the unveiling for my grandmother, I read a story that I'd written in memory of her. It was one of the few times when I felt that my writing spoke for others, about something important, and didn't call attention to itself. It performed a function – it was "useful" at the ritual moment.

A few days before Pepper died, my father-in-law came over to say goodbye to her. He is a big man, but he got down on the floor so that he could speak softly to her. Pepper was barely conscious. He told her that for all these years she'd had a job in our family, and she had done it well. Her job, he said, was to love us and to be our friend.

Beth had brought Pepper home from the breeder's a week before Ryan's third-and-a-half birthday, an occasion we were celebrating in order to make him feel special on the milestone of his little brother's first birthday. The breeder was eccentric – when she fed bottled milk to her puppies, she did it topless, she told us, because she wanted her dogs to experience the warmth and security of "fur-on-skin" contact – but she had lovely dogs, and she had just called to say she had a puppy that was particularly gentle and sensitive. The perfect puppy for our family, she said. Beth and Ryan went to her home "just to look" at the puppy, but I knew that they would return with a dog. Ryan named her Pepper because he knew that his mother had had a dog named Pepper when she was a girl. "You must still miss him," he said to her, and he was right.

I searched for something appropriate to read at Pepper's funeral, wishing that I could speak as earnestly and unselfconsciously as my father-in-law. The closest thing I found was Mark Strand's wonderful "Five Dogs" sequence, from his collection *A Blizzard of One*,[1] which has some beautiful dog-centric writing in it:

> And I stood in the midnight valley, watching the great star fields
> Flash and flower in the wished-for reaches of heaven.
> That's when I, the dog they call Spot, began to sing.

Despite much evidence to the contrary, I'd always had a sense that deep down, dogs are poetic, that they are attuned to the mysterious and the numinous. And though Strand's poem reflects this beautifully, it wasn't quite personal enough for our ceremony, and so instead we just shared our memories of Pepper. I remembered Ryan at age four sitting beside Pepper, reading her stories. All those walks. In mid-winter, in the dark of the woods at night, endless hours along the Bruce Trail and through the Royal Botanical Gardens, wandering, both dog and human, lost in our own thoughts.

Not that Pepper was always thoughtful. Yes, she demonstrated extraordinary patience as the kids dressed her up, attached her to wagons, tucked her into their beds, tried to ride her or made her wear silly hats and sunglasses. And yes, she would wait patiently outside a store when I went in to shop. But she had issues with other animals. Our lovely, quiet dog was what our family called "a killer poodle." She'd slipped her leash a few times and gone on rampages, barking and charging at other dogs. Once she'd killed a groundhog in front of a busload of Japanese tourists at the Lilac Dell at the botanical gardens. On some level, it delighted me that she was instinctive and inscrutable, a family member from another species, reminding us how difficult – and how easy – communication can be. I think of Rudi, curled up with Pepper on the couch, talking and talking about what concerned them most.

I'm sad about the loss of Pepper, but this sadness isn't only about losing our dog. I am also reminded that we have lost those times in the life of our family. My boys aren't three and five anymore, using plates as the steering wheels of imaginary airplanes. My daughter isn't a gurgling infant discovering her toes. It's almost ten years later, and though I delight in what my children are now, I have lost what they were, except to memory.

Other Happinesses: Magazines Are Good, Magazines Are Very Good

Nineteen seventy-four. Darkness. Fonts. The sheen of glossy grey Xerox paper. I, clad in white samite and sports socks. The arcane allure of a long-armed stapler, the numinous and tactile attraction of cover stock. I was ten years old and my school was having a white elephant sale. I had recently moved to Canada from Northern Ireland and I didn't know what a white elephant sale was. Our teacher, Ms. Foote – I had an intense schoolboy crush on her – encouraged us to have something to sell. So, to please her, I was going to have something to sell. And though I'd never done it before, it seemed the most natural thing in the world to write a story and make a little book out of it. I don't remember all the details, but I know *Cosmic Herbert and the Pencil Forest* was about Cosmic Herbert, an ancient and ironic wizard who had to save the pencil forest. The forest was being clear-cut by writers whose need for self-expression – and thus pencils – was insatiable. Naturally, the consequences of this were ecologically disastrous for the pencil forest and for the continued survival of literature as we know it. I don't remember how the story worked out or how my sales were, but I know I didn't move as much product as those kids who sold brownies, tank tops that they'd macraméed or little plastic statues of bedraggled and forlorn golf-playing men that said, "World's Number 1 Best Dad." But I did catch the excitement of writing and publishing. The excitement of creating work and standing behind it, sometimes literally, like at that white elephant table, or at book fairs or signing books after a reading.

Since then, I've been doing basically the same thing in various forms for forty-three years. Writing and publishing. In this way, as my favourite Louis de Bernières line says, I have demonstrated "exemplary flexibility in the face of unchanging circumstances." And how have I managed to continue this activity for all these years? To paraphrase Yeats, "I have an abiding sense of tragedy, which has sustained me through temporary periods of joy."

But today I want to talk about how vital and important writing and publishing is in all its forms, and especially how a diversity of voices, how a variety of publications – from big mainstream publishers to the non-commercial margins – is vital if a society is to sustain the cultural biodiversity needed to have a strong and thoughtful culture of inquiry, engagement and dialogue. If our society is to continue to develop and be resistant to threats – threats to meaningful dialogue, inquiry and engagement; threats to diversity and the diverse perspectives of a diverse population. Without variety in publishing, we might become like the banana industry, reliant on a single variety, a top banana which can be wiped out by a single strain of disease, as has happened before. We'll miss out on all those different kinds. Goodbye, Gros Michel. Goodbye, Cavendish.

In all their diversity, arts and culture magazines have been a central part of my life as a writer and as a reader, and so hopefully my enthusiasm and experience – if not my knowledge – will contribute something to the discussion.

The main point I'd like to make is that by creating and nourishing, by making things new, by being awake to possibility, by always examining things from different perspectives, by being the antenna of society, arts and culture *is* implicitly culture jamming. Arts and culture is inoculating. By having flourishing and varied arts and culture, we are resistant to homogeneity, to being reduced to being passive consumers of what is merely in the interests of the powerful. What is merely in the *minds* of the powerful. We can be resistant to the gravitational pull of simplifying and reductive tropes and instead have agency in constructing our world. Magazines are good. Magazines are very good.

I think of that line from the Steve Martin movie *Father of the Bride*, where they're talking about getting a videographer, and the daughter says, "Can't we just pay very close attention?"

Arts and culture enable us to pay close attention. To pay attention to *how* we pay attention. And to pay attention to *who* it is we are paying attention to.

We need to pay close attention. And our attention needs to be our own. That Steve Martin movie – well, except for the banjo – recalls the Nordic legend where Woden is attempting to beat back the circle of darkness around the world. He goes to the king of the trolls and asks what exactly is the trick for keeping troll-blackened night from eclipsing the daylight out of the non-troll world. The king of the trolls says, "I'll tell you, but first you have to give me one of your eyes."

Woden says, "Sure," and gives him his left eye. Then, "Okay, so tell me."

"The secret is," the Troll King says. "The secret is: *Always watch with both eyes.*"

Great. Irony is one of the core operational principles of the world.

I should note that this very old missing eye story is, of course, a metaphor, and it's likely an ableist metaphor at that. Everyone can learn much from those voices which pay attention in other ways and which often have gone unnoticed or silenced. Voices of people of colour, Indigenous voices, disabled voices, queer voices.

But I think this story is a kind of metaphor for, well, the human condition, and certainly also for the position of the arts. We have to try to watch with both eyes. So what do we do? Move quickly? Pay attention to the periphery? I think it has something to do with smoke, mirrors and writing really good arts grants. Also, advocacy and building community. Thoughtful writing in books and magazines allows us to resist giving away our eye, or, if we're already missing an eye, to join together and have more eyes to watch with.

I'd like to share some thoughts from my perspective as someone who works in micropress publishing and the avant-garde but also has experience with larger presses and publications.

In 2016, I was tremendously lucky to be shortlisted for the Scotiabank Giller Prize for my novel *Yiddish for Pirates*. The whole experience was amazing and took me entirely outside of my usual literary world. There I was, in a swanky room at the Ritz-Carlton, being driven to dinners with bankers in limos, stuffing myself in a tuxedo and, on live national TV, leaping onto stage before my cue – I had to stand for several minutes with Gordon Pinsent's hand on my shoulder while he delivered what was supposed to be my introduction. He was such a warm and avuncular pro that he made it all okay, despite my impetuousness. Then the week after, I was in a church hall at the Indie Literary Market, run by the Meet the Presses collective of which I'm a part, hawking chapbooks of experimental literature published by my micropress, serif of nottingham editions. I am so very happy to have both these aspects of being a writer in my life.

Some background.

In 1985, when I was a second-year student at York University, I took a creative writing class with the brilliantly laconic and insightful Frank Davey. He told us about an event downtown called Meet the Presses, a gathering of small presses devised by Stuart Ross and Nicholas Power. Davey encouraged us to create books and get a table. I did, and ended up attending both Meet the Presses and independent book fairs for the next thirty years, publishing a series of broadsheets, chapbooks and various ephemera for each event. Stuart, Nick, plus some others of us reformed Meet the Presses a few years ago to create the Indie Literary Market, so we could continue to have this home for independent publishers of literary books and periodicals. These kinds of community-based writer-publisher events, along with readings, and publication in magazines and journals, as well as the online world, have been a constant and important part of my writing and cultural life. They've been a significant part of my development as a writer and have been responsible for introducing me to many writers, publishers, friends, acquaintances, colleagues and readers, and much of the writing that has been important to me. All of which made years of engagement in the literary scene inspiring, collegial, pleasant, welcoming, intellectually engaging and fun.

As for the name of my press, serif of nottingham editions: in the manner of hair salons, I thought I needed a moniker for the press with a bad pun in it. And I love the idea of serifs – little training wheels or antlers for letters. Sudden turns in the path of the letter shape. Also, I thought "serif of nottingham" contained some allusion to Robin Hood anti-establishmentarianism.

The press began simply enough, as a way for me to distribute my work and the work of those I published, but very quickly I realized that that simple act had more complex potential. I also realized that publishing is not a neutral act. It is implicitly political and aesthetic. Publishing is part of the aesthetic of the work, in terms of its look, its distribution and how the audience interacts with the work – in terms of reading it, engaging with its writers and publishers, and in how it finds its audience.

My publishing made me part of a creative and creating community of writers, readers and publishers. Those with whom I was simpatico. Like much of publishing, it was *old school* social media.

Publishing meant that my work entered the discourse, the literary conversation. Publishing put a frame around it. It could come hot off my typewriter, my Atari 520ST computer or the photocopier at my wife's office and go out into the world. And it was distributed in a number of ways: direct contact at readings, mail networks and through libraries, bookstores, collectors, archives and book fairs.

Sometimes I played with the commodity aspect of publishing, the idea that I was creating a product that had a specific economic value.

Once at a small press fair, I sold my books by weight as if they were fish or cheese.

I also published some books in a "One Cent" edition – each one selling for a single penny. I had attached a penny to the back cover of each book. You had to give me a penny to buy the book, but in return you got a penny back. Surprisingly, I didn't sell very many. Another metaphor, perhaps. But it recalls what poet/publisher James Sherry wrote, something to the effect that "a piece of blank paper has value – you can sell it, someone might buy it, but if you write a poem on it, you can't even give it away."

Publishing in small press, I was able to set the work in a form that best suited it. A small booklet containing just one text. A single page. Hand-coloured broadsides. The design could be determined by the work. Could enter into and contribute to the aesthetic of the text. Looking back, I love how I can see the evolution of DIY publishing: from photocopied typewriting, to pixelated dot matrix printing, to Photoshop and InDesign, to laser printing and, of course, to online publishing.

Over the serif of notting-years, I have published a range of things. Mostly chapbooks but also broadsides and various ephemera (collages on envelopes, prints, leaflets, etc.). In this, I was initially influenced by bpNichol and jwcurry and their diverse publishing projects. How does writing find its physical form in the world? How does it navigate through the world and into readers' brains? How can writing be a handshake, a glance, a punch in the face or an embrace but with proper kerning?

I've also published in hundreds of magazine and journals. From tiny handmade magazines, like Jennifer LoveGrove's *Dig Magazine*, each featuring a unique collage created just for that copy, or jwcurry's *Spudburn*, where each contributor creates, by hand, each copy of their page of the magazine and the publisher binds and distributes them. And I've published in places like *Taddle Creek, This Magazine, Filling*

Station and *Grain*. As well as in places with larger distribution such as *The Walrus*, *Poetry* magazine and *Maclean's*, and online in the *Paris Review* and *Scientific American*. (They had a feature on writers and science, and I did something with butterflies, the Fibonacci sequence and ampersands.) And recently, I was delighted to have a bio in *Reader's Digest*, where I cited two past publications: *Granta* and Stuart Ross's tiny strange one-off periodical, *Dwarf Puppets on Parade*.

The opportunity these magazines gave me to try out different kinds of work, to share it with different readers, was invaluable. To find the appropriate readers for particular kinds of work. Not everyone wants to read poems that consist only of all the punctuation from Shakespeare's sonnets with all those annoying and confusing words removed. Or the story about the married couple that share a single pair of legs.

However, it's not only having my work *published* that has been important. The opportunity for my work to be reviewed and discussed has also been a significant part of my writing life, something that has helped sustain and develop my writing. Otherwise it might feel as if I'd dropped a huge boulder in a pond and there were no ripples at all. Like when I make a dad joke. Almost as if it wasn't real. Or funny.

But thoughtful discussion of my writing has taught me a lot about what I'm trying to do and what I might do next. Specific publications take an interest in specific aspects of my writing, considering the work from, say, a Jewish perspective, a historic perspective, relating it to the local or to the avant-garde, or to sharing it with readers from a particular region. Certainly, periodicals have been vital in introducing readers to my work. I can't imagine how else that might happen, short of more posts on Facebook by my mom and that big banner hanging over Yonge and Bloor.

With all this talk of the small and non-commercial, I should acknowledge that it is of course true that it's perennially difficult to make a living as a writer. My wife is a criminal lawyer, and when he was little, one of my sons would joke, "Mommy makes the paper money and Daddy makes the change."

And recently, a client of my wife's, someone who for over twenty years has been in and out of jail for petty crimes, told my wife's assistant, "Your boss's husband is one of those writer-artist types? Well, it's a good thing at least she's got a job that brings in some money." I'm grateful that this guy is sitting there in jail, thinking about our finances.

Obviously, it's important for those in the arts to be able to make a living. But it is also vital that writers and readers have access to engaging forums that exist outside of the structures of commercial publishing. Of course there is a lot of great writing that makes money, but there is also a lot of exciting and engaging writing that, by its nature and the nature of publishing, can't exist within a strictly profit-making frame-work. Smaller publications allow these writers to be published and for readers to read their work. I'd use an agriculture metaphor: commercial writing is writing that is like agribusiness, where efficiency and quantity are paramount. A lot of our food comes from here and of course it is important. However, I see the work published by smaller non-commercial publishers – and pretty much every arts and culture magazine is smaller and non-commercial, or at least exists for love *over* money rather than the other way round – as being more like family farms, more artisanal. Like organic food. Or heritage seeds. Or any one of the forty-five varieties of apples you can get at a farmers' market or the artisanal beers at a brew pub.

That sounds like I'm saying it is some kind of luxury or affectation or hobby. I'm actually saying the opposite. When the numbers aren't so big, publishers are able to take risks. To take chances. To innovate and to explore. And to allow their writers to do the same.

Maybe I shouldn't talk about this, but I've found it fascinating that, as yet, I haven't found a publisher in the US for my novel *Yiddish for*

Pirates, despite the fact that it has done well here in Canada. I've had many American editors tell me how much they like the book and would sincerely like to publish it, but they don't feel they can take the commercial risk. Some of them have said that, while they as an editor might give it the green light, their marketing departments have given it the fateful black spot.

I should note that, in light of this, Penguin Random House Canada, the Canadian publisher of the novel, *was* willing to take the risk, and so they are distributing the book in the States. So big US publishers, hear my prayer. I am a simple and honest man and only hope to please. Why don't you have as much chutzpah as your Canadian counterparts?

I only bring up US publishers here so that I can be bitter and cynical and whine a bit. But really, the point is to illustrate how big money and convergence in big publishing results in less diversity, less risk, less paradigm breaking or paradigm expanding.

I believe in cultural biodiversity and in the development of a human culture beyond the instincts of market-driven selection. Not to say that this small-scale cultural farming can't be sustainable, in a financial way – we as a society believe in supporting them in a variety of ways, including government grants. The point is that their primary reason for existing is not in order to make a profit.

I should insert here a note about my experience with larger publishers. I don't want it to seem that I'm portraying these publishing companies as if they were run by comic book villains. I mean, they publish gobsmackingly brilliant authors like me and gobsmackingly brilliant books like my novel. My experience is, of course, one of intelligent, thoughtful, supportive and kind people. The people who work in these companies are lovers of literature who understand the complex negotiations they must make in order to navigate a system that, ultimately, is determined by the needs of the corporation and its shareholders. And these people are often able to manage the balancing act of supporting books that are great, yet whose numbers keep the shareholders happy.

I see smaller publishing as more directly responding to community, and facilitating community around literature and publishing. Here, the technology of the book and, in general, of publishing is not one merely of information technology but of interactive technology. Readers, writers and publishers come together to share their "joie de livre." We can turn on a dime because we don't need thousands of dollars to continue. Our "shareholders" are people who share in our work by holding our publications in their hands, and who share our mutual appreciation of independent literature and publishing.

I remember getting a royalty statement for one of my poetry books. The publisher had taped my royalty payment to the page. One loonie, two quarters and a dime. At times like this, I remind myself that culture isn't based on quantity, but on quality. Each page isn't equally important to the culture. Take one page of Kafka versus one page of John Grisham. It's not the same, though John Grisham's numbers dwarf Kafka's.

And because it is about being sustainable rather than dominant, it's likely that some new development, some significant refinement, some worthwhile insight will come from the smaller, protected and safe-to-explore world of the smaller magazine. "Safe-to-explore" doesn't mean coddled. Often it's the opposite – the market coddles its economically dominant members. Not that big Canadian publishers don't have to be on their toes, resisting even bigger publishers from outside the country or other market forces which threaten all publishers.

The culture at large often conflates cultural relevance, quality and importance with numbers. It conflates meaning or even the penetration of a work. It confuses how many people are affected by it with how *much* each person is affected by it. And the culture often doesn't notice how many people are somehow moved by a publication's aura of influence and its aesthetic. These things are often not necessarily in the numbers. So though the number of copies measured on one axis may not be that big a number, the measure on the other axis of meaningfulness, to each of its readers and those in its cultural orbit, may be significant (and much more than a publication that has vastly huge sales numbers). I read somewhere that T.S. Eliot's *The Waste Land*, one of the most significant poems of the twentieth century, was published in an edition of three hundred that took decades to sell out.

*

I'd like to speak more about readership and community. There are thousands of specialist magazines – magazines for every kind of hobby and interest. From *Recumbent Cyclist News* to *PRO Monthly*, the trade magazine for the portable restroom operator. But something that arts and culture magazines do is create audience. Begin a dialogue. They form a readership, which bands readers together over shared interests they didn't know they had, or a shared aesthetic or perspective or set of concerns or curiosities. In this way, magazines are not only responsive to but also create community. A complex intertwining of the existing with the new.

It is significant that, as a medium, the magazine recognizes multiple forms of value. Each publication frames and recognizes different things – particular stories and particular ways of telling and representing those stories. They frame and recognize particular sensibilities. They value a particular readership, which you can be part of just by engaging with the magazine. The magazine, by its nature, speaks directly to its readership. The magazine is tailored directly to its readership. This isn't as obvious as it may seem. You can ride just by buying a ticket to ride – which in this case doesn't necessarily mean "buying," but reading, though buying is good, too. But to have a reader engage with the publication in some way – by skimming through, by noticing what the magazine considers to be worth its attention; by noticing the shape, typography, design and shape of the magazine.

The magazine enters the discourse and frames it. But the magazine also *shapes* the discourse by noticing ideas and writers who are worthy of the magazine's consideration. What? This magazine has a poem in it? This magazine is talking about experimental Inuit dance? This magazine has work by young queer femmes? It's talking about a photographic project by homeless seniors? It's talking about Hamilton, Ontario? Really? And it didn't mention New York City, Toronto or Hollywood even once?

(It does make me laugh when articles refer to Hamilton as "the New Brooklyn," or, like a recent *Toronto Life* cover, "Toronto's new hot spot.")

Whenever I teach writing, I encourage my students to make their own books, to start their own magazines. To get their work and the work of those they like out into the world. I also encourage them to find magazines and presses that publish the work of people who interest them – the students – and to find magazines and presses that will publish them as well. To develop a community of writers and readers. Having writing jump out of the typing fingers and begin a dialogue. As I said, writing and publishing is more interactive technology than information technology.

*

There are many ways in which magazines play a vital role in the creative life of our culture. Here are two examples.

I was sixteen and in first-year university in Montreal, living in a little bachelor apartment in the student ghetto beside McGill. I remember the orange carpet having the consistency of some kind of hard toffee. A really amazing jazz pianist lived next door, as well as a woman who would always get me to check for intruders hiding under her bed. I wrote a poem – it had something to do with oranges, something sexual and Boeing 747s, you know how poems are – and sent it off to *Event* magazine in BC. They accepted it. This was the first time I was published outside of school. I was thrilled to think that someone who didn't have to was willing to consider my work, to pay attention to it. I had the great privilege of having an editor invest both time and valuable magazine space in my writing. For me in my little apartment, it was hugely inspiring to think of people across the country reading my work. To think that my work was now permanently housed in this magazine. It had a home there. I was now in dialogue with readers, with other writers, with literature. I had entered the "discourse." This was a far more profound kind of *commencement* than my actual high school graduation, which I celebrated by jumping off a dock in full gown and mortarboard. Just like I entered that lake, magazines allow readers and writers to enter the discourse. They create dialogue. And my parents and I certainly had a vigorous dialogue after I got out of the lake.

Decades later, I began writing *Yiddish for Pirates*. It was the first novel for adults I'd ever written and I had no idea what I was doing. Or more exactly, I had no idea if what I was doing was working, if it could possibly amount to something. Before I'd even begun, I remember doing a reading with the writer Emily Schultz at Lillian Nećakov's Boneshaker Reading Series in Toronto. I knew Emily from the Toronto small press scene and, though I hadn't seen her for many years, we'd both published and been published in little magazines for decades. Her excellent novel *Heaven Is Small* was just out and she'd recently moved to Brooklyn – you know, the American Hamilton. We had a nice chat after the reading. So it seemed natural when I had written about one hundred pages of *Yiddish for Pirates* to send them to her and ask for some advice. I didn't really know any other real-life novelists – at least not any who didn't write crazy experimental novels – and Emily's novel was just based on the idea that the afterlife was an office building filled with cubicles. But I greatly valued her opinion, so I sent her the first half of my "monster in a box." She read a few chapters. Other than saying she liked it, she didn't offer me any feedback, but after sharing it with Brian David Joseph, her husband and co-editor at their online magazine, *Joyland*, she asked if they could publish an excerpt. That was thrilling and a great endorsement of what I was doing.

About six months later, I was sitting by the pool at my in-laws' condo in Florida drinking something with a tiny umbrella in it. I got a call from this woman called Shaun Bradley who said she worked for Transatlantic Agency. She was Emily's agent. Emily had told Shaun to check out this story about Jewish pirates in her magazine because she thought Shaun would be interested. So Shaun and I had a talk, and she said that when I'd finished the novel, she'd be interested in representing me. And so, thanks to Emily and her *Joyland* magazine, Shaun has been representing me since then, helping me navigate through the meshugen-ah Seven Seas of literary publishing, explaining the whole megillah of its Bermuda Triangles and its hidden treasures. It was Shaun who sold my novel to Penguin Random House Canada and Audible, and the French translation to Éditions du Boréal. I offer this as one example of how a magazine is part of the creative process, quite apart from simply introducing readers and writers to new work.

*

I was recently speaking with a writer-professor friend of mine, Gregory Betts, and we were talking about the entire life cycle of a piece of writing. Much of his research concerns the history of twentieth-century Canadian literature. As such, he spends lots of time poking about in archives. One thing he comes across is literary magazines, often forgotten or obscure magazines containing forgotten or obscure work. This led us to talking about how, long after the date on the cover of an arts and culture magazine, it's still relevant and, indeed, often still read. Frequently, I refer back to writing in an older magazine, something that perhaps didn't appear somewhere else, to see the writing in another context, at a particular moment in time, a certain cross-section of our culture. I run into these older magazines in my basement, in an obscure region of my bookshelves; in libraries, used bookstores or even garage sales. Sometimes, when reading a book, I follow up on the mention of which magazine the work first appeared in. There is a vast repository of scans of past periodicals online that I frequently refer to – even when I have a copy of the journal in a box somewhere in my study.

I have a copy of every journal that my work has ever appeared in. And now, with the passage of time, and hopefully due to less self-absorption, I sometimes come across these publications and see who else was in them, what the issue said about that particular moment. Also, a bit of "where are those people, now?" Until we both attended several Giller shortlist events, I hadn't realized how many times Zoe Whittall and I had been published together. I see now how we were part of various intersecting communities of writers. These magazines played a part in forming many of these communities – these intersecting circles that continue to bear fruit even today, years after the issue of the magazine.

The point is, magazines have a much larger influence over time than might be apparent. And I don't just mean in the way those old *National Geographic*s or *New Yorker*s kicking about your doctor's office do. Besides, my lawyer wife's office has copies of *This* and *Arc Poetry Magazine* mixed in with back issues of old *People*s and *Miniature Horse Enthusiast* magazine.

*

I've spoken about what magazines can do – shock, promote, encourage. They can build a community of ideas and readers. Magazines advocate not only by advocating but also by noticing, naming and valuing.

I've argued that publishing isn't a food chain but a food web – a complex network of interdependent parts of a literary ecosystem, each necessary and important to sustain the vitality of the whole. Each necessary to ensure the adaptability of the whole, its ability to face challenges and to respond to change.

When I was a teacher in a middle school, we had parents come to us filled with anxiety about what their kids should be learning, and about the future. Parents thought there were certain things their kids should know, certain ways they should be taught. Part of our job as teachers was to explain what we were doing. We needed to help parents understand that in fact what we were doing was preparing their kids. Because of the particular political climate, many parents thought some kind of quantifiable rigour, some kind of testable collection of facts, some kinds of repetitive drills and gruesome homework were what their kids needed. As a teacher, I explained how the creative, flexible, adaptable skills that kids were learning – many of those skills learned from the arts – were the best preparation. We also have to do this in the arts: explain what it is we do. We need to explain why it is important, why our approach is valuable, and necessary, even though it may appear to be going against prevailing ideological norms. We have to explain that our work is important even if it seems dwarfed by larger forces and the tremendous power of what I call "big culture." Sure, *Game of Thrones*, *Riverdale*, but also that magazine with a thoughtful discussion of an art show in Winnipeg, and that great journal with short stories from New Brunswick, and a review of a new anthology of writing from South Asian Canadians.

In the middle school, teachers worked to help the students and their parents not only understand *why* what we were doing – what *they* were doing – was valuable but also to make students feel like they were part of the process. To help them see that the process was built around them and was responsive to them. That education was a two-way street that not only suggested new directions but was built around listening.

I think this should be the case with publishing. Engaging readers by encouraging them to understand what they might not realize is of value and of interest, but also helping them understand that they are part of something, that the arts are thinking about and considering their perspective. That they are valued beyond their number, that they are a vital and integral part of the dialogue.

I remember making a little logo for serif of nottingham editions. It was a happy face with three eyes: *serif of nottingham: the alternate happiness*, it said below. I do believe that it is our role in the arts to suggest *alternate* happinesses. *Other* happinesses to those of big culture.

And by happiness, I don't only mean happiness. I mean, of course, sadness, too. I mean the full range of other responses to our world and our culture. We are able to go beyond the essentializing and simplifying. We are able to explore, as Gerard Manley Hopkins says, "all things counter, original, spare, strange; / Whatever is fickle, freckled," whatever is "swift, slow; sweet, sour; adazzle, dim"; all things "couple-colour[ed]" and "brinded."

*

I'd like to end with a final anecdote about small press publishing and distribution. I acknowledge that, in another context, we'd have lots to say about what this story reveals about the lupine putrescence of rape culture.

In the late '80s, I used to busk on the streets of Toronto. One evening, my wife and I went down to the corner of Bloor and Brunswick, in the Annex neighbourhood. I played saxophone, and a few people dropped change into my hat. But farther down the street, where my wife stood selling poetry chapbooks, several men stopped their cars, thinking that this whole poetry-selling thing was obviously a front for prostitution. It is astounding to think that anyone could mistake publishing for "Communicating for the Purpose." Publishing is so much more high risk.

"How much for such-and-such?" the men asked.

"Go away," my wife replied. "I believe in DIY."

Flying Is Just Falling
with Good PR: On Writing

1.

What is it about birds that makes me think of writing?

Is it their hollow bones, the fact that some of them can't fly?

What is remarkable about a starling murmuration is the complete shape, the elegant turns, the space each bird so gracefully keeps between it and the birds above, below, beside, beside.

Is it the sky? The egg? Or maybe it's the way the cuckoo always makes a stowaway of its egg, stashing it in another bird's nest?

Reader. Writer. Word. Language. Sky. Nest. Stowaway.

2.

Writing: A theory. Part one.

Meaning is an ostrich, head stuck in the sand – who dug the hole? – its bum-up plumage boiling beneath the sun. Its egg big as a child's head. Its legs like cancan dancers, its feathered rump like their plumed skirts.

Perhaps it is the skin and the large egg-sized eyes. What does it mean to have an ostrich appear in one's dreams, beneath moonlight, a galoot of a bird yet silent? What does the moon feel upon reflection?

What does an ostrich feel? Perhaps what a writer feels. There is space inside the breast of an ostrich for a basketball, a turkey, a heart larger than two fists, a human head.

How many writers does it take to change a lightbulb? How many moons? How many ostriches?

3.

All year, I was thinking that the branches of a tree are like birds or the flight paths of birds. Beginning with the singularity of the trunk and spreading out into the fractal bifurcation of branches. Like cracks in a windscreen or a window or like roots. The singular shattered, then reaching to the sky.

A story is like this. Or language. First there was only one thing to say. Then there were many. What was the first word, the first story?

Oh. As in, oh, here I am. Oh, I am alive. Oh, I just noticed I am alive. I just realized that I'm alive. Oh, being alive is a thing and noticing it is also a thing. And now oh is what I say when I have just realized something. Oh is the first word and the first poem. The first story and the beginning of language. Oh. My mouth like an egg. Oh.

4.

Words gather then branch, burst into leaves, breathe, gather sunlight, fall, become red or yellow and find their singular way into poems. Stories.

All year, I was wondering: How is writing like a leaf, a leaf like a bird?

If a thousand birds surrounded your head and began pecking at it, would the shield of your skull, its bony helm, fracture like an egg and reveal the naked plum of your brain to the sky?

How is writing like this? Like the bird, the shell, the sky, the brain? How is writing like the tree, or the axe being carried slowly, inexorably, on the shoulder of the forester as he leaves his little cottage, a sandwich and coffee in his lunch bag, having kissed his wife and child goodbye? How is writing like the wife, now alone, on the Internet, learning about rocket fuel and bravado, about light sockets and tango shoes, about one-way tickets to Cobalt, Ontario, where she will lead a simple life of quiet concentration and write? And burn down what needs to be burned? Build what needs building?

5.

Writing: A theory. Part two.

The eagle: I'm the best, I can fly in the air. The cheetah: No, I can run on land. I'm the best. The shark: It's clearly me. I can swim in water. The duck says nothing but smiles its duck smile.

The other day on "Twitter," I wrote a clever thing. I said, "Where there's a will there's a wild, and where there's the wild there's also a will, for wild will will will and will will will wild.

"Which is another way of saying, If God had wanted us to communicate, she would have never invented ducks."

6.

I woke up this morning wondering how is a lightbulb like a bird? It was dark, the sun was just beginning to rise, I could hear birds outside my window chirping, squawking, singing.

How many writers does it take to change a lightbulb?
One to change it, nine to think they could have done it better.

How is a lightbulb like a leaf?
How many writers does it take to change a leaf?
But why do we have to change it? the writers ask.

How are wings like a lightbulb?
How many writers does it take to change a wing?
Just one, but the lightbulb has to endure a series of conflicts and challenges before it finally changes.

How is a joke like a bird?
How many times have I repeated the same joke, or said, there's a wisecrack in everything? It's how the light gets in.
I turned on the light beside my bed and began to read.

7.

So, I'm sitting on my porch eating breakfast and the mail carrier arrives.
With the mail.
Writing has hollow bones, I say.
Or only hollowness and no surrounding bird.
Flying is falling with good PR.
Then I say, Writing is a lightbulb. How many books does it take to change?
The mail carrier looks at me, surprised, then says,
Writing is also darkness with good PR.
Writing is falling.
What happens if you fall when you're writing, like you're jumping out of a cloud, the way lightning does? Or the way a leaf plummets from the

twig? What if you fall the way an ostrich falls when it trips on a hole in the ground? What if you fall the way night falls? Or snow?

Then the mail carrier hands me a letter. I had sent it to myself. I was pranking myself, hoping to surprise myself because, after all, I am a writer. Myself.

8.

The anatomy of the avian heart. A theory of writing. Part three.

A bird's heart, like those of mammals, has four chambers. A beginning, middle and end.

There's also conflict. It's man against nature, self against society, mammal against mammal and lightning strikes and ricochets off the roof of the village church and cooks the forester, the ostrich breeder and the mail carrier equally, the scent rising like a ghost into the storm-clustered sky. In their coop, the small boys and chickens frighten and cluck, and the writer licks the nib of their quill and begins to write.

Writing inhales and squeezes like a heart, puckers its feet and flies off into the clouds.

9.

Writing: A theory. Part four.

What does writing write? Writing writes writing. Writing writes the unwritten. Birds, by virtue of being birds, write of un-birds and the flightless. This is like writing. And also birds.

I write of birds. You could say, I bird my time. The sky is filled with flight. The land with flightless birds. Birds like ducks float. The night is crammed with what isn't day. The day allows us to write of the night. Inside the night it's too dark to write, but when one changes a lightbulb one sees like a bird.

Wittgenstein writes, "Whereof one cannot speak, thereof one must be silent."

But one can change this "cannot" with writing; one can use writing to explore this whereof and thus change the thereof.

Existence may precede essence, but writing proceeds. And it precedes the way a mother duck leads her ducklings. Whereof something swims, walks and quacks like a duck, thereof it is a duck. Or a viable duck simulation. Someone replaced my heart with a duck and I never realized. Not until it rained.

10.

Who's on first, but What is the theory of writing.

What can one write of saying? What can one say of writing?

It's like flying with bad PR.

So, like falling then.

So, write again and fall.

Fall again. Fall better.

Even silence has something to say.

Some bird has just or is just about to sing.

Yes, and: The Ampersand, Twenty-Seventh Letter of the Alphabet

A few years ago, the burger chain A&W unveiled a new logo to mark its centenary and placed itself at the centre of a simmering linguistic debate. The new logo looked a lot like the old logo, except for one omission: between the *A* and the *W*, in that familiar brown italic font, was – nothing. The ampersand is under threat, the company suggested in an accompanying press release. Once recited as part of the alphabet, the character with the preternatural ability to couple is now not only frowned upon by editors but also considered too perilous even for the Internet, where it can't be used in a hashtag or URL. And that matters to A&W, not least because the ampersand is the conjunctive meat in the Mama Burger of their name. Thus, the tongue-in-their-onion-ring-filled-cheek campaign demanding more respect for this "useful, universal symbol of bringing things together" and the Change.org petition the chain created to support the ampersand's return to the alphabet. "In this digital world, its exclusion has made all of our lives a little harder," the petition stated, and more than seven thousand signatories seem to agree.

The ampersand seems a natural symbol for our emoji-driven age. Indeed, there's a brilliant Reddit thread that bewails the fact that it isn't one: "There's literally an ampersand on the category icon for symbols, yet there is no usable ampersand emoji." You click a virtual shift key that includes the ampersand symbol, but only other symbols are available. "And?" you might say to yourself.

The idea of a letter – at least from a Western alphabet – having special qualities, eliciting a particular affection, belongs, perhaps, to a different time or to an ancient culture: a time of sigils and runes, letter-like forms that invoke magic and demons. Jewish mysticism conceives of the letters of the Hebrew alphabet as having existed before the world itself and believes that the world was created out of these elemental letters. This tradition also imagines the shape of the letter as a kind of visual allegory. The letter aleph, for example, points to heaven above and earth below.

What is our relationship to such alphabetic signs now? We live in a world of texts and tweets, emojis and keyboards. We experience and respond to our environment through text. The way we read the world these days, it might as well be made of mouse-draggable objects like clip art or symbols. Maybe, without knowing it, we have all developed a complex tactile, emotional and conceptual relationship to letters. But are we losing our intimate connection to them – to the ampersand – because of the digital? We rarely write its Möbius shape. Our view of the world changes when we are warm while no longer felling trees, splitting wood, making fires in the hearth.

I've always been fascinated by this sarabande of a symbol, this conjunctive flourish, this curliest of wand paths: the ampersand. It looks like a letter while not actually being a card-carrying letter; at least, not anymore. It's a knot that lassos both + and *and* while deriving itself from the joined letters of *et*, the Latin word for *and*.

And I'm not alone. *Canadian Art* explains that artist Iain Baxter& was "so in love with this most curvaceous, twisty-turny piece of Anglo type" that he "legally appended it to his own last name." And ampersand-thusiasm fills social media with the kind of fetishizing connoisseurship that endangered things attract. Think of steampunk or handlebar mustaches. We're living in the ampersandthropocene now. Throw pillows, T-shirts, jewellery, tattoos and entire social media feeds are curly-toed for the ampersand.

The ampersand used to be a kind of twenty-seventh letter, included at the end of students' recitation of the alphabet. That's how the symbol & got its name. Students would say "per se" ("by itself") before any letter that was also a word in itself (e.g., *A* and *I*) to indicate that they meant the letter and not the word, and that included the symbol for *and*. They would recite "and per se and," which soon became streamlined to "ampersand." Though the symbol has been around for a long time – Keith Houston in *Shady Characters: The Secret Life of Punctuation, Symbols & Other Typographical Marks* notes that it was used in graffiti in Pompeii and remarks that the AD 79 eruption of Mount Vesuvius does "impose a rather hard upper limit on the possible range of dates" – *Merriam-Webster* dates the first use of the name to 1795.

I'm attracted to the ampersand because of its shape. It's a miniature mother & child – the mother embracing her child, their conjunction – but also a kind of Möbius strip, a twisting ouroboros. Yet, like a Hebrew mystic, I want to read it symbolically: it is time turning back on itself, but it also links one thing and another, a joining. The cover of my book *For It Is a Pleasure and a Surprise to Breathe: New and Selected Poems* has an image where an ampersand takes the place of the heart. The heart joins. It is an *and*.

About fifteen years ago, another typographic element, the semicolon, was popularized by Amy Bleuel as a symbol of suicide survival because it's "used when an author could've chosen to end their sentence, but chose not to. The author is you and the sentence is your life." The ampersand is symbolic, too, but one that is less specific, more mysterious.

Paying close attention to the text we use is part of being sensitive to the highly communicative culture we live in. We need to watch for signs. We need to consider them critically but also creatively. A letter shape has a speed, a weight, a personality. It is the shape of our thinking, of metaphor, of our concepts. Text is a kind of musical score; a score for thinking. We need to see the big picture but also examine these very small pictures, because, ultimately, they reflect our selves. "&" we need to continually ask ourselves, "&?"

Three Sides to Everything

1.

In this essay I will. "In" this essay implies an inside and an outside, some kind of boundary. As if the essay were a Boston cream and its filling a payload made of words. But the essay is both inside and outside. Or at the very least, an inside and its skin.

Some years ago, when I went to see an internist, my son said that every doctor who isn't a dermatologist is really a kind of internist.

A dictionary is a hole in all the words it isn't.

And an essay is a hole in everything it's not. Strange how the puddle is the exact size of the water as well as the hole. And what's this duck doing here?

But this essay hasn't been written. It is, as they say, early days. And these early days – the sun shining in the front room, the dog curled beside me on the couch, some guys outside in reflective vests doing something to our street – aren't part of the essay. Yet.

What is it to have lost many relationships with friends and family? There's the presence of their absence. Lost for many reasons. Time, distance, death, illness, disagreement, hurt. I'm a hole in everyone I'm not. Or everyone is a hole in everything that isn't me. Certainly, these losses are holes in me, holes that are not just empty but filled with loss. It doesn't feel like relationships are ever truly gone, rather they are replaced with these feelings.

We know who we are not only because of our little dog but also through the broader triangulation of all our relationships, both past and present. Some are still active, and some continue in the way of half-lives, still radiating. An essay is its words just as we are our relationships. An essay is also the words it is not (see relationships).

I've also lost many of the ways that I've thought and experienced life. I've lost my former self in many ways, but I've gained this other, this Gary 59.0 – I'm fifty-nine as I write this – always a Beta version, functioning with a few glitches, but for the most part operational. The earlier operating system no longer functions as it once did. It's changed. I've had to acknowledge that some things are lost. Or weren't how I thought they were. Or, in some cases, hoped they could be. I create meaning by what I'm not, this trace that I'm formed around.

We lost that third boy we expected to have – we thought we'd seen him and his boyhood on the ultrasound, but a girl was born instead. We also "lost" our nephew in the very best way – she'd been a niece all along and it was our great delight for her to finally be able to be herself. But these aren't losses, and certainly not griefs but happy replacements – futures we didn't anticipate but celebrate and which entirely eclipse the world we once thought we'd have. Did I imagine being in Hamilton, Ontario, for the last thirty-three years – was that my future? No, but even so, my life fits me like a puddle. In this scenario, I'm the water or the hole. The duck.

Like the dictionary, I'm choosing to gather, to notice, to record and consider only some things and leave out others.

2.

When I went to see an internist – because I was feeling exhausted – he asked me a series of questions that were clearly about determining if I were depressed. In his lilting Irish accent, he asked, "And so what would you do if you won the lottery?" I had just returned from a family holiday in Ireland where we stayed at a charming cottage near the Cliffs of Moher. "I'd move with my family to County Clare and buy that cottage and spend my time writing." "Ah no, for much of the year, County Clare is too rainy and cold, it's Tuscany where you want to be. There you'd be, in a villa on a hill, and all those travelling by would point up at you and say, 'All those novels, how does he do it?'"

Tuscany or County Clare, I'd take either. Burnt umber and sunshine, or mist and deep green. Or Hamilton, Ontario, where no one walks by pointing at me and my ostensibly productive novel-life.

I read about how to insert filling into a doughnut. The usual cake-style doughnut isn't appropriate, rather you need to use a yeast-based rising doughnut, so that there is a hollow inside. Then it is simply a matter of using a cream-filled pastry bag with "a small round decorating tip (a Wilton #12 would work well for this). Poke a hole in the side of each doughnut and fill with pastry cream. The doughnuts should be served as soon as they are filled. They are best the same day they are made."[1]

The Mexican writer Valeria Luiselli cites an "unknown genius" in the epigraph to her essay on Joseph Brodsky: "There is nothing more productive or more entertaining than allowing oneself to be distracted from one thing by another."

I imagine taking a "donut" and inserting the extra "ugh" like orthographic filling, plumping it up like asides such as this one, filler perhaps, but enjoyable if you like that kind of thing. Sometimes almost the entire point

3.

There are friends that I haven't spoken to in decades yet still consider friends. School friends, old girlfriends, those who more rightly might be considered acquaintances. I watch for news of them on social media or more directly, through mutual friends. Why haven't we spoken? Sometimes distance, opportunity, change: they might have a lack of interest or consider we've "grown apart." A few because of a disagreement or bad feelings, but not mine. I tend to feel that once I've made a connection with someone, looked "into their soul," as it were, however provisionally, it is impossible to stop knowing them, or in some way to stop caring about them. How deep is the commitment? In truth, it is more a feeling than action. There are those I feel this connection with but still do little to interact with them. So many souls, so little time, energy or organization.

4.

My in-laws' friends are dying. This is also my parents' experience, though they speak about it less. They all are in their eighties, as are most of their friends. As a consequence, the news is often about cancers, heart attacks and strokes. Sometimes after years of struggle, sometimes shockingly suddenly. They no sooner hear about a diagnosis than a few weeks later, they learn that their friend has died. My mother-in-law used to joke that her mother-in-law, who lived until her late nineties and seemed always to be attending funerals, only went because of the free food. Last night she said, glumly, that she now understands. Three friends had died this past week. Her life is filling up with funerals, never mind free food.

I remember the days when it seemed all our friends were getting married. Then a few years later, having children. Then the ups and downs of careers and children, and now a wave of retirements for our older – or luckier – friends: teachers, crown attorneys and so on. Also parents getting sick or dying. Announcements of children getting married, grandchildren being born. Our friends getting sick. I see where this is going.

My parents and my in-laws have friends that they've known for seventy or more years. Despite immigration, the world changing, families realigning, war and illness. When my in-laws chose to renew their vows in a beautiful backyard COVID-complicated ceremony attended by their children and grandchildren, my father-in-law's very ill best friend managed to attend. They'd known each other since they were boys. Sixty years before, he was one of the witnesses to their marriage. How moving that he was able to once again witness his best friend's marriage sixty years later, before passing away soon after.

5.

Mid-afternoon and the light is pearlescent, the sun shrouded in clouds. I'm back in the front room with the dog curled beside me. I'm not eating doughnuts but hamantaschen, the traditional Jewish triangular Purim pastry. Though the pastry is usually dry and isn't, shall we say, exquisite, it's eaten because the three-sided shape recalls the three-sided hat of anti-Semitic villain Haman from the Purim story recounted in the Megillah. Eat the rich. Destroy the pastriarchy. Sometimes the filling is jam – apricot or prune are big favourites – but I'm having my favourite: poppyseed paste. Is this supposed to represent Haman's slurry of a villainous black brain inside his hat? Is it a lesson that hate can taste good, or that victory and schadenfreude (in this story, the Jews won) can be sweet?

6.

It was someone's Bar Mitzvah and there was a room under the bimah. The bimah: the raised stage where synagogue services take place, where there is the ark for the Torahs, the podiums for the rabbi, and the cantor and place for others involved in the ritual. Sarah and I were both twelve and we went into that room beneath all the adults and kissed. It was the first time I'd kissed anyone or was kissed, except for that one awkward time when I was seven and the down-the-street-lady kissed me on my neck and, with her perfume and warm wet lips, got me worked up, some combination of excitement and shame. But Sarah and I kissed. The next day, we tried to go to a movie on the bus but discovered the movie we wanted to see wasn't playing. I don't remember what happened next, but that was the last time I saw her. Later – ten years? – I heard that she'd died in a car accident in a snowstorm. When we kissed, I was too young to know what I felt, but now I look back on it with kindness, sorrow and compassion for this girl, this tender moment we had – one that, slight as it was, I still think about, this early learning. Two kids sharing such fragile tenderness, delicate and sweet.

A doughnut is an inside, an outside and a hole, which can be inside or outside, depending. Almost everything has an inside, an outside and a between.

But why doughnuts? Because of pleasure, the discursive and discussed below, the Jewish pastry used as a euphemism for the female Garden of Eden, to paraphrase Noel Simon.

7.

Jean Cocteau wrote that "a great literary masterpiece is simply a dictionary in disorder." But a work of literature doesn't use all the words of the dictionary. Is it possible that by looking at the parts of the dictionary that were not used, you could reconstruct the literary work? The work is both the words that were used and the words that were not used.

By knowing something about the hole, you know something about the doughnut. More and more, I'm figuring out who I am by figuring out who I'm not.

It's a kind of dead reckoning, a system of navigation that doesn't rely on absolute position but on figuring out where to go and where you are by measuring the distance and direction from where you've been.

Who I am is both inside and outside my life. In my life. Around my life. Through my life. During. Despite. Because of. What, I wonder, is the apt preposition?

MEAT AND BONES

The skeleton wasn't in the closet. It was hanging in my father's study. A human skeleton. There was also a shelf of fetuses suspended in liquid. Animal fetuses, though I thought they were human and that one was my elder brother, if he'd been born. I knew my mother had had a miscarriage before me. My father was a medical student and then a doctor.

But I didn't find these things strange or macabre. They seemed natural. Just part of my dad's work, part – or parts – of all of us. It was the equivalent of listening to music and then seeing the instruments. Or listening to language and knowing it was made up of letters. Bodies as signs in the language of living.

*

I made these artworks: the pelvis is half bone and half butterfly. The hip is a bone wing. A *W* is also a kind of pelvis, hippy and with spaces where other things go. There's an actual *W* wedged in the pelvis. I hate it when that happens.

I make these things because there's magic in transforming the body. Making with words, with the letters of the body. The idea that the world is made of the body but also we are embodied, made of our body with all its archives of injury, pain, joy, pleasure. Its stories.

*

Remember those anatomy illustrations in the encyclopedia made of layers of transparent pages? Turn a page and the skin disappears. Turn another and the nerves are gone. Then arteries and veins. The heart. Lungs. Other organs. The last page was the bones alone. More naked than naked. It ain't no sin to take off your skin and dance around in your bones. Then like playing a movie backwards, you could reclothe the body in itself, gift-wrapping the self in its own skin. Then finally, close the encyclopedia and clothe the body, front and back, in encyclopedia pages. The book was a bed or a coffin for the naked body.

*

Things I've seen. The inside of my wife's gullet and stomach. The inside of my own. The inside of my own alimentary canal. My bum. Endoscopy. Colonoscopy. I've seen scans of my wife's brain. Of her uterus. Ultrasounds of our babies still as embryos or fetuses. What my teeth look like inside, their roots, dark spots. I know how flexible my liver is (not flexible enough, according to my gastroenterologist). I've seen my fractured spine after a car accident – a hairline fracture in C2, the vertebrae second from the top. (I discovered in psychology 101 how unbelievably fortunate it was that it was only a hairline fracture at my literal hairline.) The subluxed disc around my lower spine, thankfully cut out. Once they searched for one of my testicles with an ultrasound. They couldn't find it. Apparently, it was "floating," a buoy, a dolphin, a message in a bottle.

*

In writing and art, the body is made of parts. It can be taken apart. Never mind that it is always someone's body. There may be feelings involved.

*

In earlier times, we didn't know what was inside the body. At least not when we were still alive. It was like what was in the sky beyond what the naked eye could see – those crazy moons of Jupiter – or what was deep below ground. We knew bones because they remained in our remains, but our insides were like the distant places of the world.

*

Making art, I often conceive of the parts of the body as signs or images, language or icons. A pair of legs walking on their own. A head separated from the body, still speaking. Lungs as the wings of a butterfly. An image, half ribs and half brain. Hands instead of the head of a deer.

Until something is wrong with an actual body. Pain. Injury. Disability. The skull and crossbones were someone's skull, someone's thigh bones. Something happened to the flesh that surrounded them. This flag is about that. Beware.

Perhaps exploring the body as a constellation of signs teaches us by contrasting it with our experiences of actual bodies. It unpacks the assumptions within symbols, signs and icons. The toe of St. Somebody-or-Other, the thigh of the blessed Otherperson. The reliquary of our body. An ossuary of thinking. What have we encoded and what encodes us?

*

When I was young, I learned from my father to long for perfect moments, iconic scenes with their textures and tones just right, part of an identifiable script, platonic forms of a life or lifestyle. These were what lay beneath reality, the potential, the "bones" of the matter. Mood, atmosphere and emotional heft expressed in unfolding time; in words, light, objects, interactions. Sometimes attained, frequently aspired to. I'd try to arrange things just so. Coordinate props and sets. Light a fire. Have the appropriate clothes, books and music. I felt the powerful bittersweetness, the beautiful melancholy for the nostalgia of what could be, as if the present was a kind of remembering or recreation. As if I were a historical re-enactor.

*

One night I walked out of my high school dorm room and saw what looked like actual stardust sifting down through the air. It wasn't possible. It was magic. This was the wished-for, dreamed-of beneath-the-surface, a Platonic form realized. Revealed. Eventually, I figured out it was a trick of the streetlights, the light covered in inverted pyramids, which created this effect. I was disappointed. Relieved. Disappointed. Maybe I'd have to do the work myself in this world.

*

How unhappy-making was this narrative: wanting life to become nar-rativized. Storified. And sometimes wishing for events to occur, both good and ill, so I could have the deliciousness of the protagonist's pos-ition, as hero or victim.

*

It took many years for me to learn to experience what was there, what was actually unfolding in front of me, something that could be newly experienced because it was the first time rather than the enaction of a template. This isn't even mindfulness, but allowing the messy flow of the actual. This isn't the same thing as seeking the more authentic lurking beneath the skin of accepted convention. Perhaps it is simply the struggle between the Platonic and the materialist actual, the ideal versus the phenomenological.

*

I was sixteen and went to visit my girlfriend in a different city. She'd baked a heart-shaped pie. Things were going to be "so beautiful they'd hurt." I went to the washroom. I flushed. The toilet overflowed. Shit flooded the room, and because there was a hole in the floor, it rained down from the ceiling of the floor below. My shit flowed over the clean laundry and all over the room. In *Slaughterhouse-Five*, Vonnegut writes, "Everything was beautiful and nothing hurt." This wasn't war, but I was a teenager. My girlfriend's older sister cleaned everything up.

*

I think about how we literarily develop in response to the world, how we become what we think and feel. The world becomes encoded in both the physical structure and the physiology of the brain. When we learn language, our brain changes in a certain way. As we learn to walk, our brain follows. A new pathway, a developed neurological structure. Then this organic ever-changing "innernet" goes on to colour our experience.

*

We visited a cemetery in Cuba with our sons and daughter. The grave-digger who guided us plucked horny goat weed from a grave and gave leaves to me and my sons. Then he laid his open hand against his other elbow and bent the arm up. The universal sign for a sproingy erection. He showed us graves that were glass-fronted room-sized mausoleums showing the former life of the deceased as single rooms: a child's bed-room, a doctor's office, a youth's room with a motorcycle smashing through the wall (for he had died in a crash). Then he led us to the os-suary, boxes of bones stacked on shelves. He lifted a stone lid off one and handed my son a skull. We have this picture, my son, surprised, his big curly hair a flourishing bush around his head. The unexpectedly small yet adult skull resting in his hand. The broad smile of the gravedigger.

*

I'd like to think that when someone we know dies, they don't disappear because our bodies have encoded them in its structure. We may not see them, but we see with them. They are (in) us, in our way of being, in the honeycomb of our self. Not that I don't feel as if a team of burly men were tug-o-warring on my nervous system, attempting to haul it and the weaving of memory out of my body, but maybe I can see if I can find the one I lost in my body, not only in its ache but in its structure or in the shape of my thinking, the texture of my perceptions. I may hurt, but they are always with me; are, in some ways, literally part of me.

*

A doctor friend described looking in a small girl's ear. Spelunking with one of those little lights they use to illuminate the inside. The girl's mother, sitting beside the girl, was patiently waiting to hear what the doctor saw, what was the cause of her child's discomfort. I looked, my friend said, and there was an eye staring, gazing unblinkingly back at me. Okay, I said to myself, I'm the doctor. I must be calm. I must try to understand what is here, what it is that I am seeing. She looked again, trying to be dispassionate, but the eye continued to stare at her. It shone like glass from the narrow aperture. Glass, my friend thought. A doll's eye. Somehow, this girl has a doll's eye, pushed like a pea up a nose, deep inside her ear, looking out at the world through the aperture. Looking straight at the doctor, wondering what she would do now.

Writing as Rhizome: Connecting Poetry and Fiction with Everything

I sit down to write this on a snowy Monday, the sun bright, the air cold. I begin this like I begin most things: without having any idea what to do. Without having any idea where I'm going. Also, I may have been too ambitious when I wrote that subtitle about connecting poetry and fiction to *everything*.

Everything?

Okay, so I won't say anything about my liver. Except for just then.

But in truth, beginning with knowing nothing and having only a vague sense of expectation and a willingness to explore is a good place to start. It really is the state in which I begin most of my writing. Also, how I fill out most of my tax returns. Besides, everything is connected. It doesn't really matter where you start. As my son once said, the first five syllables of anything is the beginning of a haiku. And I do want to talk about how everything is connected. How everysome is elsecome thing.

But look how I just started from somewhere, from not knowing, from just beginning anyway, and here I am almost at the end of the first page, the first minute or two of you reading. And things are beginning to unfold. To suggest possibilities and directions. To paraphrase an old chestnut from Robert Frost:

Two roads diverged in a yellow wood.
I took one.
It doesn't matter which.

I'm not giving it back.

I do want to talk about writing from a place of not knowing, from a place of discovery, exploration and play. But first let's talk about eyebrows.

During my first years of being a middle school music teacher, students would sit in the back of the class and do this kind of salute thing, dragging single fingers across their eyebrows and then pointing them forward while saying, "Connect. Connect." It took me a while to figure out what they were doing. They were making fun of the fact that I have, what in the technical language of middle school is called "a unibrow." My eyebrows are one. They connect. Me and Frida Kahlo. After I realized what my students meant by "connect," I began greeting them with this unibrow salute, and they would salute back at me.

Connect. Connect.

This shared and ridiculous act connected us. It was a kind of "knock knock, who's there" call-and-response. Me and language. Me and my students. Kyrie eleison. Christe eleison.

A friend of mine, Robert Majkut, once called me up from work. He'd asked someone what his job was. The guy had said "Courier Liaison," and so Bob had immediately responded "Christe eleison," but the bon mot was lost, and so he called me up so I could put it in this essay.

But let me say more about starting from nowhere – about trusting the process, trusting the language and your own response to it.

When I teach, I often tell my students, "The writing knows more than we do." What I mean is that language is a vast repository, a great archive, a word hoard, a storehouse of accumulated knowledge and experience. Everyone who has ever used those words is there in the language. Or is pointedly not there. Language can be a Stolperstein, a stumble stone. A marker which remembers, which reminds; which draws your attention to time, place, history, culture – to the world. Just by virtue of being a speaker of the language, you have access to this knowledge. You have access to something much larger, much deeper than just yourself. You're a tree connected to the rest of the forest by its roots. Or maybe you're a leaf on a tree, connected to a twig, connected to a branch, connected to a trunk, connected to a system of roots, which connects you to the entire forest. And as the song goes, the green grass grows all around and around, the green grass grows all around. And you *can* see the forest because you're a tree. You're an antennae upside down and in the ground.

I'm saying that language is its own internet. I'm saying that we should trust where our writing is taking us. Listen to the writing. To our own words. To the rhythms, the images, their associations. To how characters speak and what they say. Maybe you can feel it in your body as you write and – especially – as you read what you have written aloud.

You don't have to know what you're doing. You don't have to have a plan. Writing is an exploration. You can figure it out as you go along. You can start with a plan or a direction, but it can evolve. "The writing knows more than you do," and by listening to it, you often discover things that you didn't expect. Things that were much more subtle, interesting and complex than your original idea, yet somehow express what you didn't know you were thinking or feeling. It can lead you to greater and more emotionally rich writing. It's good not to insist on what you thought the writing was going to be. It's like a parent insisting that their kid be who they want the kid to be rather than allowing the kid to discover who they are.

I'm also saying that you should trust your own language, your own particular place in the language. And maybe ask how it happened, how you became rooted in this particular place. Like a tree, as poet John Terpstra says, you're the expert on the place where you stand.

But I also want to make clear that at the same time that language isn't to be trusted. Or at least, we shouldn't trust its silver-tongued, inky-black, duplicitous illusions to be more than a delightful play and ploy of signs and wonders. It's the rope that isn't there, yet that gives us enough length to hang ourselves on our hope that we might be able to pull ourselves up by our own bootstraps. To throw a line between ourselves and our minds, our minds and others. As much as language is a tool for discovery and empowerment, it can also be a tool of deception, suppression and silencing.

Interesting writing comes from our engagement with language and how it pulls us and how we feel its pull and either go along with it or resist it. How we negotiate its energy. And by language, I don't only mean words, grammar, phrases, sentences, paragraphs and so on, but images, stories, tropes, themes and structures as well. I mean how we interact with an audience through publishing and what assumptions we make in general in our literary culture.

What if a tree falls in the forest and there's no one around to hear it? It's a forest. There are other trees. Other living things. They hear. They can hear the sound of the trees that have fallen in the past, the anticipation of trees that will still someday fall. And they can hear the sound of the network of trees itself. That's language.

Writing is connected with everything.

Once I wrote a haiku for the late poet David W. McFadden:

Why do we worry?
Every word on earth is
in the perfect place.

There was something about representing both ironically and yet at the same time earnestly this – hoped for, imagined – felicity of words and feeling. In my next poetry collection, I revised the haiku:

Do why worry we?
Word every earth on is
in place perfect the

The play with the hoped-for had become more self-referential. It had become a more compromised and contingent dance, something I saw in many of my favourite McFadden poems. I was trusting the language, but interrogating it more intensely.

But before we talk about everything else, let's stay a while longer with uncertainties, mysteries and doubts, without any irritable reaching after fact and reason, as John Keats says. Negative capability. It's what my gym teacher always said I had.

You know that song about the bear going over the mountain to see what he could see? I think that interesting writing often comes from doing what I call "the Bear Method."

This is how it works. Like a bear, you look to see what you can see – that is, what is the most interesting feature on the fictional landscape. That mountain over there? That's definitely the most interesting thing around. So you head for it. When you get to the top, you do it again. You look out to see what you can see. What's that? Oh yeah. It's the next mountain. And then you head for that. And when you get there, you survey the next valley to see what you can see. I think you get the picture: you write your way toward something interesting and then when you get there, you decide where you should go next. You can't plan because you don't know where you're going – you don't know where you expect to get to or how you're going to get there, but you go, confident that your mind and imagination are always the best tour guides, are always able to connect your writing to the most things. And of course, if it turns out that the mountain isn't interesting, you can always go back and head toward another one. It isn't like cutting out the wrong bit when you're a brain surgeon. You always get a second chance. You still can have an idea of what your ultimate destination might be. Here's an example.

When I wrote my novel *Yiddish for Pirates*, I knew that my

protagonist, a Bar Mitzvah boy from Eastern Europe, would become a pirate, because I wanted to write about Jewish pirates. And because he was a pirate, he would eventually search for treasure. But what that treasure was, I didn't know. I also knew he'd search for the Fountain of Youth. Because ... pirates. Also, it was rumoured to be in Florida – perfect for the Catskills shtick of this Jewish pirate. I also knew that he'd travel with Columbus to the Caribbean because some Jews did. In fact, Jews were expelled from Spain in 1492, exactly when Columbus sailed the ocean blue. Coincidence? I think not.

Actually, it was a coincidence, but did you know that Columbus brought a translator who spoke Aramaic and Hebrew with him, in case they ran into one of the lost tribes of Israel? "So, how have you been this last two thousand years?"

When I began writing *Yiddish for Pirates*, I thought about who might narrate it, who might be there to observe all that piratey stuff. Then I realized. Of course, a parrot would be the perfect narrator. It sits on a pirate's shoulder and observes everything, like a GoPro camera. And like a Greek chorus of one, it can comment on the action and make sarcastic asides. As I like to say – and as I like to repeat because I think it's so clever – there's a wisecrack in everything. That's how the light gets in.

And parrots learn the language of whoever they are with, so this Polly was a polyglot. But parrots (at least ones that speak human language) have to use the limited language they know, the limited language they have received – the words, tropes and stories – to express their reality. To mediate between themselves, their thoughts and the world. And to question whether this language is expressing their reality or constructing it. This is just like human beings. Or writers.

And then I read about the explorer Humboldt who at the end of the eighteenth century came across a South American indigenous village that had been entirely destroyed by war. There was no trace of its people or its language left – it wasn't a written language – except for one parrot that had flown away from the village and knew about thirty words of their language. The language survived because the parrot was a kind of a dictionary, a book. So Humboldt wrote these words down and was able to figure out the meaning of many of them since the parrot used them in context. And then I read about a contemporary artist who had taught modern parrots to speak this language. From parrot to parrot, this language, this way of seeing the world, this world view, was passed down. Like with books.

And like with Yiddish. I wanted my book to be filled with Yiddish because it carried the culture, the humour and the way of being in the world of Ashkenazi Jews. And so my parrot spoke Yiddish. Maybe the narrator is the original parrot who sailed with my pirate and Columbus, or maybe that parrot passed his story down to another parrot, who passed it down to another one and so on. The parrot is like a book.

By the way, I read about domestic parrots in Australia that escaped into the rainforest and taught the wild parrots how to swear like sub-urban Australians, but maybe that's another thing.

I had called my main character, the boy who becomes a pirate, Moishe, which sounded like a good name. It is the Yiddish for Moses. I knew I could do lots with it regarding exile, the Promised Land and the rest of the Exodus story. Then I thought about what to call his parrot, the narrator of the story. Well, if the protagonist is Moishe – Moses – the narrator could be Aaron. If you remember, in the Bible, it is Aaron who speaks for Moses, so that seemed perfect.

And so, this is why the parrot who narrates *Yiddish for Pirates* is named Aaron. Actually, he turns out to be a five-hundred-year-old im-mortal Yiddish-speaking parrot. Aaron swaggers around trying to be as macho as the pirates in the story because he's learned language and culture from the pirates, and thus their grammar of gender. In the heart of the book, I was writing a scene where Aaron meets another parrot. It's a hot parrot sex scene in Yiddish with lots of *ach ach ach*s and *oy oy oy*s. And, in the middle of this, Aaron, the parrot, discovers that he is gay. I had no idea that this was going to happen, that my own character would come out to me as I was writing him. But I feel that by listening to my story and its characters, by trusting that the writing knew more than I did, I ended up with a much more interesting character. And a more interesting book. I had to wait until my characters were knee-deep in their own made-up lives before *I* knew, and *they* knew, what they would do next. In retrospect, it seems obvious that the parrot was gay, but I really wasn't expecting it. Maybe he wasn't either.

That was a long way of illustrating how to trust the process of writing. How one thing can lead to another. How everything is connected, and if you are attuned to the possibilities inherent in what you are writing, the possibilities that you uncover as you research or think about your writing, you can be led to really interesting places. The brain reaches out like a root system and we hear the resonances, echoes of our own place in space and time, in history and in the world. I imagine how we look into space and see constellations. We make imaginary yet powerful connections between stars – we see patterns and stories between things trillions of light years apart that somehow hit our eyes at the same time.

And because all of this is our process, this process of discovery will be connected to us and to our sensibilities, even if we don't know it at the time. I should also say that the process of making a mistake or happenstance can also suggest a new path, if we read such a thing as an unexpected possibility, a serendipitous opportunity. Something about integrating randomness, exploring the dynamics of the creative material or process or just your mother. I mean, a fruitful Freudian or Jungian slip.

For me, regardless of whether I'm writing text, or music, or creating visual work, I try to attune myself to the shapes, sounds and patterns

– to trust the process, to trust that the materials will speak to me, that the material and I, the process and I will enter into a conversation. And I think that the not knowing, the bewilderment, the feeling uncertain and finding it all difficult and sometimes just hard work, I think of it as ultimately drawing out greater depth and sensitivity from me and my process. When things are less easy it forces me to go deeper and to look beyond the oblivious and the obvious.

I have to remind myself of this one hundred times a day, when I'm dissolving into a sea of self-doubt and distinctly un-Hemingway-like anti-bravado.

But another thing I want to say. If someone gives you some writing advice (like I am doing now), but you've got a better way, or a better idea that works for you, do that.

Now before we really roll up our sleeves and talk more about connection, about other ways in which writing is connected and connects, let me offer a few lines from Juliana Spahr's powerful long poem, "This connection of everyone with lungs":

as everyone with lungs breathes the space between the hands
and the space around the hands and the space of the room and
the space of the building that surrounds the room and the space
of the neighborhoods nearby and the space of the cities and the
space of the regions and the space of the nations and the space
of the continents and islands and the space of the oceans and
the space of the troposphere and the space of the stratosphere
and the space of the mesosphere in and out.

In this everything, turning and small being breathed in and out
by everyone with lungs during all the moments.

It's a beautiful passage. We're connected by breath. Everyone on Earth shares the same air. It does, however, make me think of air mattresses. An air mattress as some kind of a book that holds the exhalations of whoever blew it up. A song or poem of the breath contained within the mattress. At least it's better than that dream I had where a woman was sleeping in a waterbed and pulled back the sheets, and there was her ex-husband in scuba gear, watching her from inside the waterbed.

I called this "Writing as Rhizome," and it occurs to me (okay, it occurred to me five pages back, but I was busy talking about something else) that I haven't spoken about rhizomes directly, though I've been circling around the idea.

So what's a rhizome? About two pounds.

Actually, a rhizome is an often unnoticed connection between things, an invisible network. Trees communicate rhizomatically through their roots. Fungus colonizes the roots and passes chemical messages between them. The wood wide web. A rhizome is a network with no centre. It's formed of connections between things. As cultural theorists Deleuze and Guattari write, it "has no beginning or end; it is always in the middle."

As a writer, imagine being in a circle whose centre is everywhere and whose circumference is also everywhere. You're like a spider in an infinite web that, because it's infinite, has no centre. You feel the trembling of the twilight-coloured filaments. Something is with you on the web, somewhere. Imagine language having no beginning or ending, but being like an endlessly extending, endlessly expanding mind map. The Earth is also in the non-centre of an expanding universe. Maybe one of many. An infinite number of particles and waves wash over and through us. But maybe it makes more sense for you as a writer to imagine being outside every circle at once.

Writing is a rhizome. Language is a network of connections. Words. Grammar. Stories. Sounds. Rhythms. And it grows rhizomatically the way root systems do, searching for the most nutritious paths, not having a pre-established plan beforehand but rather "seeing what it can see."

Writing and publishing is a network of communications. Wherever you are, you're both the centre and also there is no centre. Or the centre is everywhere. Which means you can start anywhere. And your voice is as much the centre as anyone else's. Sorry, Shakespeare. Though of course, we can learn a few tricks from the old Globe spinner.

This is my call to arms. Or rather, my call to Word. Because there is no centre. We can use writing to explore, represent and construct, and we don't have to accept the gravitational pull of received notions of the world and reality. We can speak our reality. We can make our own.

It reminds me of that protest chant:

What do we want? A time machine.

When do we want it? It doesn't matter.

Writing is a microscope and a telescope, antennae and tentacles, but it's also DNA. But DNA that we can use to create the world as we see it. The texture and sense of being in the world, the sense of thinking in the world, of using language in the world, that is ours.

Before I'm done, I want to talk about my last novel, *Nothing the Same, Everything Haunted: The Ballad of Motl the Cowboy*. When I was writing it, it wasn't the only thing that I was working on. I find it energizing to work on a few things at once, so I always have multiple projects on the go. It's good when you want to procrastinate to have another thing to sneak off to work on. Shh. Don't tell my novel, but I'm going to the coffee shop to write some poetry. And shh, don't tell my poetry, I'm sneaking off to the library to work on some music. And shh, don't tell either of them that I'm sneaking home to watch Netflix. It's for research. Really. I mean, which character on *Friends* is really into Wittgenstein? Is it Joey? *Whereof one cannot speak, thereof one must be silent. How you doin'?*

While writing *Nothing the Same*, I was working on three books: a book of selected poems, a book of poetry that I wrote with poet Tom Prime, and a CD and book combination that I created with poets Lillian Allen and Gregory Betts. I was also working on a couple of chapbooks and a couple other collaborations, as well as some musical performances and a proposal for a public art installation in Hamilton. I tell you about these things not because I want you all to think I'm so clever and productive – but aren't I just so clever and productive? – but because I want to talk about the messy, rhizomatic organization of creation and a writing life. Sometimes it's being alone in an undershirt with an old typewriter and a bottle of whiskey in a cold water flat in Brooklyn, but more often it's a complicated and vibrant process, weaving your writing into the whole range of emotions from exhilaration to boredom. Weaving it into the many other things that you do at work, at school, with your family and in your life. Like research on Netflix. Maybe it includes the strange compulsions, revulsions and inspirations of social media. Reading. Watching. Listening. The negotiations with who you are and what you want to write, what you can write, what you feel you should write.

Collaboration has been a big part of my writing life. It's exciting and fun to work with others, and I love the experience of getting out of my own head and trying new things. I find it very freeing. Not only do I learn from how the other writers work but also I often discover another way that I can write or think about writing. And, to be honest, there's something about the work not being all about me, about not representing "me" alone, but sharing the responsibility for authorship with another. Encountering another's world. Attempting to understand what it is they experience or value necessarily expands your own writing and your ability to think creatively.

It also focuses you more on the process, on the writing itself and on the dialogue, the interaction.

Last night, Tom Prime and I were working on some new poems. He's in Victoria and I'm in Hamilton, so we Zoomed and worked together on a Google doc. For these poems, we both are writing and editing the text at the same time, so by the time I get to the end of a line, Tom may have changed the beginning of it. The manifestations of our creative processes exist in continual flux, and we have to continually adapt and be flexible. We are very different, but the process results in lots of energy. As well as surprise and enjoyment. I met Tom while I was writer-in-residence a few years back at Western – he was an undergrad who consulted with me. Over the years, we've become peers and have ended up writing a couple of books together. He's currently working on his Ph.D. and shares all sorts of mind-blowing aspects of his research in our ongoing collaboration.

I've been arguing for improvisation, for a process of educated guesses, for the willingness to change and be flexible. Through writing we grow new senses. We grow new connections within ourselves and out there in the greater world.

Ursula K. Le Guin wrote that "the imagination is the single most useful tool mankind possesses. It beats the opposable thumb. I can imagine living without my thumbs, but not without my imagination."

Yes!

I believe that writing and storytelling, poetry and fiction, as a subset of imagination are also some of humankind's great technologies, some of our great tools. For investigation. For community. For keeping on keeping on. Our writing tells us we may not know the plan, we may not have a plan, the world might not seem to have one either, but somehow, we're in this together. Everything is connected. Or to use the Latin, *To Everygether Nected Con Is* and together we tell our stories from beginning to our end.

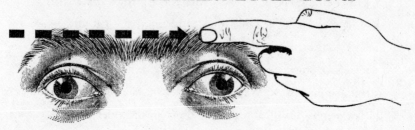

TO EVERYGETHER NECTED CON IS

On Between

1.

Cell walls? I'm against them. Also, divisions between things. Between physical objects. Between people. The separations between things are, in some ways, working fictions. Yes, there are different "zones," but I have this notion of everything being part of this huge protoplasmic unity. From galaxies to the insides of dogs and the undersides of sweat socks. Air, our lungs, birds. Ash. Fire. Turnips. Do we really need cell walls? Don't worry, scientists and cellular creatures, I'm speaking mostly but not entirely metaphorically. Because don't things morph into one another, if only eventually? The same is true of concepts and abstractions. One person's manbun is another's mantra. Is it true that someone's pain is my pain and it is only the self and society which create reasons to keep them at a distance? I want my thinking and feeling to reflect the fundamental unipanrhizomatubiquity between/of things.

2.

I often walk in the woods around Hamilton. There are surprisingly many trails, waterfalls, forests, cliffs and winding paths. I love wandering, not knowing where I'm going. When I walk on a trail system and accidentally discover how it's connected to another system, I'm a bit disappointed. Some of the mystery, the potential, is gone. Things seem a bit smaller, both conceptually and physically. The possibility for association, for resonance, for imagination, is reduced. I want to discover a myriad microcultures, microworlds. I don't want to believe in base ten. I want to believe in base infinity. I like the opportunity to be a flâneur through a non-repeating labyrinth.

3.

All connections are pataphysical. All categories. Even the number two is one.

4.

Yesterday, I was walking through the woods listening to poet Natalie Diaz speak about empathy in relation to sympathy.[1] She says that you can't actually feel what someone else is feeling. You can sympathize, you can find analogies in your own experience, but the particularity of their feeling in relation to their identity, experience and the processes of their being are not something that you can actually feel. Of course, this doesn't mean that you can't feel compassion and connection, but, she says, it is important to note the distinction.

5.

Dolphins are "the second most encephalized beings on the planet."[2] We are (add heraldic trumpets and showers of confetti here) the first. But their brains are not like ours – more folds and ridges, a smaller hippocampus. And ravens, crows and other corvids' brains are even more different, yet show clear signs of intelligence. Recent papers in *Science* show that crows "know what they know and can ponder the content of their own minds, a manifestation of higher intelligence and analytical thought long believed the sole province of humans and a few other higher mammals."[3] The scientists have found an "empirical marker of avian consciousness."[4] It seems that consciousness and intelligence are more about patterns of connectivity and activity in the pallium, the most neuron-dense part of a bird's brain. Neurobiologist Suzana Herculano-Houzel writes that "brains can appear diverse, and at the same time share profound similarities."[5]

6.

It's been a long-standing thought experiment of mine to try to imagine the world from the perspective of a medieval person or a Neanderthal. This is called "writing," you might say. Not that the brains of people from other times are so different, but my main efforts are trying to feel their sense of self in relation to community, the individual, time and geography. In this regard, I often return to the Borges' story "Pierre Menard, Author of the *Quixote*." Like Menard, who ends up writing as if he were Cervantes, except that he is living in the nineteenth century, even if I could attain access to the minds of historical humans, there'd always be a kind of double consciousness (to brazenly appropriate W.E.B. Du Bois's concept from *The Souls of Black Folk*). The thoughts or writing of another time have an entirely different meaning in their new context. Salt is entirely different when in pickles or in coffee. I'm aware of my twenty-first-century brain and its particular experiences and formations. How aware? You'd have to ask my therapist.

7.

It's often said that a dog has the intelligence of a two-year-old, or that a dolphin has a seven-year-old's brain, but the nature of their intelligence, their awareness and processing of the world, is fundamentally different. Not only in terms of simple things like a dog's vastly more sensitive sense of smell or a dolphin's echolocation (not to mention its life in liquid), but surely the nature of their thoughts. Their experiences of the world are profoundly different than that of humans. I imagine a shiny silver ball bouncing around a pinball machine – lights flashing, flippers flipping, *Charlie's Angels* and starburst images lurid and worn. That's a thought. A thought implicitly has context. A different brain would have a different pinball machine. Two levels. Mr. T imagery. A square ball.

Made of moss. Seven flippers and the entire thing filled with water. Can a thought exist independent of a mind, or other thoughts? Phew.

What would non-human thoughts be like? What is the awareness of a tree, listening through the chemicals of its roots, the actions of its leaves? A sap telegram? Can we have "tree thoughts" without a tree body, or at least a "tree mind" developed through the engagement of what the tree has physically engaged with?

Okay, and now to try to think like a triangle. Not the *Flatland* kind, but to think of nothing but three sides, three angles, an inside and an out. Damn. I accidently considered depth. Ah well, we'll always have hypotenuse.

8.

The other is an infinite labyrinth, not a maze, though there have been those relationships. I want to connect but not know. Knowing, thus, is a collaboration.

9.

Can there be connection without identification? Aren't we all stardust, anyway? Almost all of the elements were formed in stars. So yes … except some of our almost 10 percent hydrogen content may be even older than stars. Thirteen to fourteen billion years ago, the Big Bang created helium, hydrogen and small amounts of lithium. (What is small when we're talking the entire universe? Where on the breadbox-to-supercluster continuum is it?) These three Legos are the OG of elements. And eight-track tapes. So at an elemental level, we *are* connected, literally made from the same stuff. But the devil – in this case individual humans or groups of us – is in the details: there's about 0.1 percent biochemical difference between humans, but I still wouldn't mistake Napoleon for Lupita Nyong'o.

Can I feel what my sister or brothers feel? My children? (Just ask them: no.) I can care about, act with compassion, understanding, relate to and so on. However, on some non-trivial level, I can grasp that we have the same relation to the larger world, to many smaller worlds also. There aren't the exact words to express this. I can "commiserate" without actually feeling the same thing. I can imagine standing in their shoes if they have shoes, if they have feet. I can imagine them standing in their own shoes and me in mine, and both of us standing on the same road, in the same landscape, on the same planet. There is something profound in this fellow feeling. There is something profound in knowing we are different yet stand together. This love between us – how can it be anything else but love, whether we don't know them, like them, kinda hate them or have "feelings" about them? We are here together. We are made of the same stuff and will return at the end of our lives to the same state, a whole mess of Big Bang–created energy and matter.

10.

Okay, it can feel like something other than love – I have this one neighbour ... – but, of course, I'm talking about getting outside the daily view, seeing the big (or infinitesimally small) picture. I'm not here to minimize struggles for justice, fairness, safety, sustenance, health, basic needs or security. Those are difficult shoes to stand in. Maybe this all sounds trite or like a truism, but the world is as the world is, the universe, too. An incontrovertible fact. A quiddity – a thisness. What to feel in the face of this inherent entanglement, this betweenness? Gratitude, awareness, perspective, awe, fear, overwhelmedness? Equanimity, bitterness, unfairness? Love, triangularity, the electromagnetic force?

11.

But let's talk birds. They exemplify betweenness. Cloud to cloud. Tree to sky. Wingtip to wingtip. Murmurations. They have hollow bones.

Everyone knows it's to help them fly. True, but it's not to make the birds lighter. They need so much oxygen their bones are an extension of their lungs. There are air sacs in the hollows. And birds breathe in oxygen during both inhalation and exhalation.

12.

Birds fly in what they breathe, like fishes in water. But we humans – and I assume it is humans reading this – however else other creatures think, seem uniquely able, because of our particular brain, its cortex, its folds and ridges, to imagine cohabitation and commonality with each particle and each force in the embiggening universe of which we are made.

THAT'LL LEAVE A MARK

Some artists hope their work will make them immortal, that they will live forever through their art. In his Xenotext project, poet Christian Bök has been attempting to make a poem by modifying the DNA of an "extremophile," an organism that can survive in such extreme conditions that, even after the heat death of the sun, both the organism and the poem will survive. Some writers publish their work in flyers, leaflets and booklets – what is termed "ephemera." These might not survive a supernova, let alone the recycling bin. Then again, who would be around to know?

One day I accompanied my friend Gregory Betts, who was going to the Rare and Special Books Collection at the SUNY at Buffalo library. Since the organizers knew I was coming, they took out all of my "ephemera" in their holdings for me to sign. I don't know where they got these often quite rare artifacts made for readings, book fairs and for distribution on lampposts, bulletin boards and to friends. Certainly not from me. I found it profoundly moving that somewhere in the world, someone had carefully collected these publications of mine, works I'd created from when I was eighteen. To think that these fragile bits of paper were carefully catalogued and preserved in plastic envelopes for "posterity" or the heat death of the sun or the end of funding, whichever came first. I also realized that if they had my work, they also had, in addition to manuscripts by headliners like James Joyce, thousands of other works by small fries like me, all archived to record the rich and varied story of literary production.

Yesterday, someone emailed me to ask if they could use one of my artworks for a tattoo. I love the idea. It is a kind of publishing: both very permanent (it is, after all, a tattoo, ink buried into skin) yet temporary (how long would this person live? Perhaps longer than the presses publishing my work and certainly longer than my books would remain in print). It is an alluring metaphor for the relationship between art and audience, between writing and reader. Oh, that'll leave a mark. Was it Kafka who said that? Well, something like that in "In the Penal Colony."

The tattoo makes me think of the reader "wearing" the work, being marked by it. They have skin in the game. The work and the experience of it (their choice of work, the implied experience of reading it) literally embodied on their skin. We write on the surface of paper. By some process of sympathetic magic, the skin is turned into page and the writing appears there. Shelley Jackson's the SKIN Project uses the publishing space of the skin of volunteers who each consent to have a single word of a novella tattooed on their body. Only those who receive a tattoo are permitted to read the entire story. It makes me think: if one of the volunteers dies, it's a form of radical editing, of redaction. The story is only kept alive by the combined life force of the volunteers. And fate. Unless the words are passed down parent to child, loved one to loved one – I bequeath you this "the" from the middle of the story. I also think of all the word-wearers as lining up in order or alternately forming a mob, a text in disorder and possibly angry. Perhaps they reorganize into a different story. Part of the novella is the invisible grammar of sentences, the narrative organizing them. The tattooed readers could rebel. Resist. Rewrite.

A couple of years ago I, along with two artist friends of mine, Tor Lukasik-Foss and Simon Frank, was chosen to create a public artwork for the City of Hamilton. The work was to address refugees, migrants, immigrants, persecution, the search for freedom and safety in new home. We designed and had cast ten bronze suitcases with a variety of symbols on them. One suitcase would lie open on its side with a live tree growing out of it. I'd never been involved in creating public art, let alone sculpture. The lengthy and expensive process of creating bronze sculptures was fascinating. High temperatures. Fire. Blowtorches. Chemicals. Molten metal. Here was a work that I was involved in that was really heavy. Literally. And permanent. It could last for hundreds of years ensconced beside the path in the park. Not at all like a leaflet.

Another significant difference for me is that unlike with most of my published work, there is only one of this sculpture. There is an "original." All my other works exist as multiples, editions of at minimum a handful. The notion, at least for most of my writing, is that the work is an idea, regardless of its beautiful material manifestation – gorgeous paper or cheap photocopies, design features, stitching, page-turning choreography, cover illustration. These are, of course, often very significant aspects of the work – many poems use the form of the page, the interaction of the reader, the movement of their eyes and hands, how the light falls on the paper – but for most literature, the work exists as a gathering of words in a conceptual space. The page, the made marks of letters, are just carriers of this abstract language. Even a work like Aram Saroyan's famous "eyeye," though it relies on typographic sleight of hand, is more about the abstract system of orthography – the idea of letters and spelling, and how they are related to the object invoked or evoked. There is no original.

The SKIN Project attempts to circumvent the abstraction of writing by having it embodied on the skin of humans. And with only one copy of each word marked on each living person.

Certainly, the novella exists independently of its material manifestation. Jackson must have had, at least at one point, a typed version of all the words of the story. The tattooed words, though unique and unreproduced, rely on the abstraction of the organization of the novella. What makes a dictionary into a novel? It's not just the words. A dictionary is literature in waiting. An archive of linguistic potential.

Which brings us to Walter Benjamin's essay "The Work of Art in the Age of Mechanical Reproduction." What's the difference between a unique artwork (an original) and one produced in multiples, likely by mechanical reproduction? What's the difference between the *Mona Lisa* and a poster of the iconic work? One difference that Benjamin refers to is "Aura": "The authenticity of a thing is the essence of all that is transmissible from its beginning ... to the history which it has experienced. Since the historical testimony rests on the authenticity, the former, too, is jeopardized by reproduction. And what is really jeopardized when the historical testimony is affected is the authority of the object. One might subsume the eliminated element in the term 'aura' and go on to say: that which withers in the age of mechanical reproduction is the aura of the work of art."[1]

Do our suitcases in the park have this aura? I'd say the aura of public art feels different to that of art in a gallery. Maybe this is something to do with how public art becomes part of the daily experience of a neighbourhood. People walking their dogs or with their children. Birds fluttering down. University students having a coffee. That guy who graffities LSD on everything, even trees. Various people putting their hands in the handles of the suitcases and miming carrying them. The work becomes part of the psychogeography of the place and time. Like in Murray McLauchlan's song "Down by the Henry Moore," it becomes a landmark in an urban experience. There is a way in which literature can become part of an urban experience. For example, arriving in New York for the first time, I couldn't help but filter my experience through all the place and street names I'd read for years in books. During the roaring winter dusks of Brooklyn, I sit in a dive on 52nd Street. I would rather look at you than all the portraits in the world, except possibly *The Polish Rider*, occasionally, and anyway it's in the Frick (Ginsberg, Auden, O'Hara). But you don't (for the most part) sit on literature, or run your fingers along it. Birds tend not to splotch on books, except for the most critical avians. The idea that work could become part of the scenery, absorbed into the daily life of citizens is fascinating. But also, that they might continue to experience it in different ways, if only to notice some new detail or change, to wonder again about what it might "mean." This is, perhaps, a kind of ambient aura that is specific to place. Even if something were mass-produced, it might have a particular and unique relation to place. Benjamin: "Even the most perfect reproduction of a work of art is lacking in one element: its presence in time and space, its unique existence at the place where it happens to be."[2] Yet it is still uncommodifiable. It has limited transactional value except for the price of its materials (and we'll be solidly securing the work into the ground to thwart would-be metal salvagers).

It's been three years since we began the project, and due to many things – COVID and bureaucracy among them – the suitcases are not yet installed. They wait in a storage locker like lost or unclaimed baggage. Along the way, I've joked that documentation of the tangle of institutional processes would have made a better artwork than the actual art. The numerous surveys of the land (and the negotiations between public and private ownership or operation), the various procedures, reports, policies, documents, insurance policies, invoice and payment tangos have been both telling and fascinating. Does the process have an "aura"? Could it even be reproduced? What would its documentation look like? Perhaps it'd be its own kind of operational *Arcades Project*, à la Benjamin's unfinished book, what was to be his extensive compendium of the arcades – the covered alleys – of Paris? Is this process a kind of grammar of the physical art-work? Does it tell us more about the nature of citizenship, governance, public policy and a society than just a few hollow lumps of bronze? What does it mean that the process isn't commodifiable though the artwork is (unless the process was documented and made into a material object somehow)? Although everyone involved is paid, the monetary value of public art doesn't work exactly as that of other art. It can't ordinarily be bought and sold. Like writing. The only way to commodify a particular instance of published text is to have a rare edition or manuscript copy. The actual "writing" floats outside materiality, not quite a Platonic form but a shadow in the head nevertheless.

NFTs. Pfft. By recreating ownership and rarity even in the digital world (you have an actual certificate), and exchange value (you have to buy them, even if it is Bitcoin and not doubloons, cows or gold bars), NFTs are creating another kind of "aura." I'm not exactly sure what this digital aura is – it's a complicated construction based on traditional art, digital reproducibility, licensing and the assertion of ownership of what is much closer to the idea in literature. The NFT is a between-space of not quite limited material object and not quite idea. Maybe it is something akin to the mechanical rights of a performance versus the copyright of a song.

A work of art isn't (usually) a suitcase for carrying its contents. The suit-case is the content. In writing, is it the potential hand on the handle, the possible traveller and their route? We walk along holding a suitcase that isn't there. That's the writing, though maybe we travel with (i.e., read) the suitcase for a time. Unless, of course, the writer works to problem-atize this. I remember in the '80s, bpNichol showed me one of his *First Screening* computer poetry works, where as you read, the text you have just read begins to change. What you encounter in reading the text is the experience of reading.

There's the physical art object and then there's the experience of the object. The aura is part of the experience of the physical object. There is another kind of aura in literature: the aura of reading the authentic actual work even though it is eminently reproducible. Here I am, reading this particular vision of the world. Here it is and here I am with it, and not anywhere else, even though the work has no meaningful physical presence.

Recently, I heard book artist Annette Le Fort speak of the relation between the book and the hand. We hold books in our hands. We turn pages, we touch their surfaces. Verso and recto are like wings or two hands. The size of books is often related to our hands. We close a book as if it were two hands in prayer, open it as if to receive. I think also of a book's relation to lungs, both left and right, and also to the two lobes of the brain. There may be many copies of a book, but there is only one of us. What is "original" is our experience.

THE ARCHIVE OF THESEUS

When I think about personal libraries, I don't imagine the Escher-like metaphysics of Borges' infinite library, Alberto Manguel's bookish temple of bibliophilia and erudition, or even the imperial force and nostalgia of that remarkable picture of Joseph Campbell surrounded by George Lucas's English manor-house hero-of-a-thousand first editions library on his ranch in California. I think of my grandparents' bungalow in Nepean, Ontario.

When they moved to Canada, one of the first things they did in their new house was to knock down a wall between two rooms so that they could install "their library" – their large book collection with its dark wood shelves and Persian rugs. There I read about everything from Noah and his three sons to four-armed Nataraja dancing within a circle of fire; from Kafka's Josef K to the Ship of Theseus, replaced board by board. Each book in their library was carefully catalogued by my grandmother. I would look through the various dictionaries, encyclopedias (Jewish, historical and philosophical), the older editions (leather bound, bearing the marks of hands, of reading, of travel, of time), the collections of many or all books by a single author gathered together on a shelf (I imagined where my books would go, in their place on the *B* shelf) and the bookcases of Hebrew and Yiddish books, obscure to me, but their unintelligible whispering and humming was a mysterious and affective ghost.

My grandparents' interest in Jewish learning, in the mystery and value of books, language and knowledge for itself, caused me to consider that each corner and crook of the world was filled with story, with knowledge, with thought, with words, with opinion. My grandfather had an interest in bon mots (frequently his own) and Jewish jokes (frequently his own). There was a sense that through knowledge – manifested via the conduit of books and a personal library – the world was larger and had roots.

He was also a polyglot. (Man, he was hard to clean up after – ask my grandmother.) He was not a religious man, but he was fascinated by religious texts and knew Hebrew, Afrikaans, English, Yiddish, French, Russian, Lithuanian, some German and bits of other languages. I remember arriving late one night to find him with about five different bibles open in front of him, comparing the texts. My grandfather and I would go to the local library once a week when I was between ten and thirteen. I'd read random things that caught my fancy – books about madrigals or haiku – while he read the Israeli newspapers in English and Hebrew.

A characteristic memory of my grandmother. Sitting in her green chair or lying on her bed with a book (library-wrapped by her in plastic) – mostly frequently a contemporary or classic literary novel – reading with a dictionary beside her. She was a fastidious reader, always careful to check on unfamiliar words or usages. She also told stories, mostly during those times when my grandfather wasn't there to interrupt or eclipse her. Those quieter times between things. There wasn't the sense of having an audience (in both meanings of the word) that there was with my grandfather, or of tagging along on a particular project or enthusiasm that he'd been seized with. She'd talk while baking or while I helped her walk from a chair to the dinner table (which, as her arthritis took hold of her bones, could take enough time for a story or anecdote).

All of my grandparents were migrants, emigrants, wandering a varied diaspora of Jews, living in a diaspora of memory. Often Jews feel like they are a diaspora of themselves, living in the past and in the future, but with complicated feelings about the present. And so they live in language, a place that is there and not there. Its palpable sensory reality is present, is here, yet always refers to something else. A sign of relief, of regret, of hope, of expectation, of witness. Their personal library.

*

What about *my* cohabitation with books? Unlike the well-ordered collection of my grandparents, that served to reinforce, preserve and establish – though part of me longs for such a Talmudic colloquy with the traditional structures of inquiry – I wish for my own library to surprise and confound. To afford me the chance, as Dylan Thomas says, to read "indiscriminately and all the time with my eyes hanging out."[1] My personal library isn't in one place. It's pervasive. It's scattered. It oozes. It's environmental. It's in most rooms in the house. On shelves. In stacks. Beside the bed. In the bathroom. In books borrowed or ones that have wandered off to friends and family. I think of it as rhizomatic. Connected in invisible yet nourishing ways. From book to book. From book to me. And from book to my now adult kids. They have some of the books, as indeed, I ended up with some of my parents' books, as I still think about the books they had in my childhood. To paraphrase a discussion about Deleuze and Guattari's notion of culture, the library "spreads like the surface of a body of water, spreading towards available spaces or trickling downwards towards new spaces through fissures and gaps ..."[2]

Is my library about social capital and display? About possession? Completism? Collection? Delight? Rigour? Hierarchies of knowledge and power? Is it aspirational? I suppose to be honest, some of that is inevitable. However, I think of one of those ball pits for kids. I'd like to jump into a room of books and roll around. Writhe. Play. But, y'know, with the mind.

My daughter used to challenge me to describe the location of one particular book out of the thousands we own. I'd surprise myself by being able to specify the shelf and the place on that shelf even though the books were not organized alphabetically or by subject. This reveals to me how my books are always on my mind. They reveal a particular topography of my knowledge or thinking. Which includes hidden corners. Things I didn't know I didn't know. Or that I hadn't realized I thought about or believed. Or that I once did. What was forgotten. What was imposed. Accumulated. Stashed or lost. Back to that discussion of Deleuze and Guattari: "Rather than narrativize history and culture, the [library] presents history and culture as a map or wide array of attractions and influences with no specific origin or genesis, for a '[library] has no beginning or end; it is always in the middle, between things, interbeing, *intermezzo*' (D&G 25)."[3]

Japanese has the term "tsundoku" for unread books in one's collection. I wonder if there is a term for a book that one has had in one's possession for years and years and then finally reads? There's something revealing about this. What the book once represented, what it represented as a familiar, an icon, a relic. What unlocking its uncommunicative presence might reveal. How was expectation different than realization? I'm okay with having books that I never read. They are physical representations of world views, of a way of being in the world, a way of addressing the world. The Greeks had the idea of a memory palace, an imagined place, a physical representation of mental phenomena. A personal library is a kind of palace, too, though not only of memory but also a topography of mind or potential. More than a palace, it's a garden shed.

My library is a record of my reading or my thinking about reading. Of communities – writers I know or identify with; readers, thinkers and enthusiasts I connect with; bodies of knowledge shared; cultures and times. My library is a collection of books read, to be read, to be noted; of writers witnessed, supported, protected, shared. Of hopes for the future. My library takes the shape of memory but also the shape of how I imagine the world or, better, how I imagine imagining the world.

Books are mile markers. Talismans. Familiars. Touchstones. Goalposts. Survey markers. Signposts. Though there are those books which wandered in, one way or another, and stayed. An unpleasant guest who signed a guestbook. Who left a book or left a space where one was.

It is precisely the disorder, the ramshackle non-hierarchical clutter of my library that is its value. It is a non-linear retrieval and storage system for memory, knowledge and culture. Like two Escher hands writing each other, my library is an affordance. A quantum archive of an autobiographical imaginary. The library "'ceaselessly establish[es] connections between semiotic chains, organizations of power, and circumstances relative to the arts, sciences, and social struggles' (D&G 7)."[4]

I hope my library can be speculative, to have the same relationship as speculative fiction does to realism. It's not the library of Theseus, because I never throw out the old parts. It's a Thesean archive. Where have I been? Where could I have been? Where am I going? Where could I go? I don't need a map, or the new same-old boat. I have this library.

Sunshine Kvetches of a Little Parrot[1]

A rabbi, a priest and Stephen Leacock walk into a bar.

Wait, Stephen Leacock says. How did I get into this joke?

Don't worry, says the priest. You'll get used to it.

It's true, the rabbi says. And in these jokes, we always walk into a bar. But I've figured something out. The bar is our lives. It's a metaphor.

Oh right, says Stephen Leacock. Of course. Then what's the punchline?

Exactly, says the rabbi. That's the joke. We don't know.

*

Since the Leacock Medal celebrates humour in literature, I'd like to take the opportunity to share some thoughts about the surprising and seemingly unrelated topic of humour in literature. In Yiddish, "to kvetch" means to whine or complain. So, in honour of the parrot narrator of *Yiddish for Pirates*, my friend, writer Stuart Ross, told me that I should call this "Sunshine Kvetches of a Little Parrot." Brilliant.

*

I have just returned from a reading tour of China. I had a conversation with a Chinese interpreter about how she translates humour from English to Chinese. Sometimes, she said, the humour is untranslatable, and so when she interprets, she explains to the Chinese audience that the author has just told an untranslatable joke. And then she asks them to please laugh now in order to respectfully acknowledge it.

I think from now on, I'm going to use that for all my readings. Whether or not you think this is funny, I'll ask you to please laugh now, to respectfully acknowledge my attempts at humour.

*

We humans have discovered many things. Fire, language, agriculture, roller skates. War. Kindness. Art. And humour. Humour is one of our great technologies and it has accompanied us on our evolution from ape to Facebook user. Certainly, other animals have humour – a chimpanzee can appreciate the classic slapstick of a fellow chimpanzee slipping on a banana peel as much as the next hedge fund manager – but I think it is only we humans who see humour as saying something more.

Though life may be difficult, we can always take heart and watch people slipping on bananas. We may ourselves wipe out on a banana, but there is something satisfying about recognizing how in falling, we partake in "the human condition." Though there are others we might wish would partake in this human condition more than us. Though we may despair, we can always laugh together as the powerful and self-important slide to the ground. It's hard to worry when you see how ridiculous things can be.

Ultimately, humour is philosophical, metaphysical, spiritual, social. There must be a version of the story of Adam and Eve where before they ate the Forbidden Fruit, one of them first slipped on its peel.

There's an old Jewish story that I love:

A man goes to a rabbi and asks if he can explain Judaism to him while the man stands on one leg. The rabbi sends him away saying, "Don't insult me with your ridiculous gymnastics." Next day, the man asks the great sage Reb Hillel to do the same thing. Explain all of Judaism while he stands on one leg.

"Left or right?" Hillel asks.

"Either. Does it matter?"

"Tell you what, you jump in the air, and while you're there, closer to God, I'll explain everything," the sage says. "Ready? Jump!"

And what does Hillel say when the man leaves the ground? He says, "Do unto others as you would have them do unto you."

"That's it?" the man says as he returns to earth.

"That's it," Hillel says. "The rest is commentary."

This is both a joke and a revitalizing reminder. And just like the best humour, it cuts through all the commentary and pretension, and, ultimately, anxiety-producing complexity. And it's memorable.

*

Humour gives us distance, and also an opportunity to deal with difficult things. Jewish humour, in particular, has a kind of optimistic pessimism, or pessimistic optimism, that is an integral part of the culture. There's an old saying, "We laugh to keep from crying." And Yiddish writer Sholem Aleichem (on whose stories *Fiddler on the Roof* is based) wrote that "Where there is laughter, there is hope."

We laugh because it gives us an alternative to despair. There's an old joke –

Why don't Jews like to drink?

Because it dulls the pain.

Life may be difficult and there may be pain, but it is our own pain. We claim our right to define our own experience on our own terms. We may not always have had land, or power, or money, or rights, but we always have had the ability to frame our experience. To claim it as our own. Perhaps to connect it with all others who have experienced adversity in other places and at other times. To look tragedy in the eye.

What's worse than finding half a worm in your apple?

The Holocaust.

It's a terrible joke, but the point of it is that instead of being driven to despair and hopelessness, we can look it in the eye. This isn't about minimizing life's struggles, it's about not allowing them to be in charge of our life, if only for a little while.

Through humour, we are able to stand outside what's happening and look at it philosophically. Through humour, we find a way to engage, to think about what is happening and still have agency. Many times, humour addresses things we can't change, and even if we can't change something, humour always gives us agency because we are telling the jokes. Or we are the one to whom the joke is told. That's a very powerful position from which to address pain, anxiety and tragedy.

I think of the following line, sometimes attributed to Spike Milligan: I'm not afraid of dying. I just don't want to be there when it happens.

Humour is a way to keep going. The narrator of Samuel Beckett's *The Unnamable* says, "I can't go on. I'll go on." Through his own awareness of the absurdity of life, and of his own absurd position in this absurd life, he finds a way to go on.

I love Beckett's dark and revealing humour. In his play *Endgame*, a character tells this old joke:

A guy needs a pair of pants and so goes to a tailor. The tailor tells him to come back in four days. The guy comes back four days later.

"So sorry," the tailor says. "Come back in a week."

In a week the guy returns, but the pants are still not ready. "Come back in a month."

This keeps going until finally, at the end of three months, the tailor brings him in to pick up the finished pants. By this time, the guy has lost his patience. "It only took God six days – six days – to make the world. And you, you took three months to make me a pair of trousers."

"Yes, but my dear Sir, my dear Sir, look ... at the world ... and look ... at my TROUSERS!"

Humour not only helps us to manage our expectations and to take agency, it also builds relationships and community. If you tell someone a joke, you're sharing a perspective, you're in this together somehow. You're seeing something together. Even if you're only imagining telling the joke to someone, you're still reaching out and making a connection outside of yourself. You're imagining fellowship and community.

Humour can dissipate tension or enable us to re-examine power relations. This is humour's jester-function: to speak truth to power, to reveal, to open up what is hidden or not spoken about because of power, convention, tradition or ego. Often, it says what can't be said another way. It is socially sanctioned dissent. Or to use Drew Hayden Taylor's term, "permitted disrespect." It allows us to see that the emperor's new clothes are all sizzle and no steak, all hat and no cowboy, and we see the naked truth – maybe in the emperor's case, too much of the naked truth.

Humour is revitalizing because it allows us to see what isn't seen because of routine or convention. It calls out what we take for granted – both to critique and to appreciate. Maybe our own foibles or the foibles of our society. Humour is a tool to cause us to look at the world differently. It deconstructs assumptions and unexamined tropes. It "makes it strange," as Russian literary theorist Viktor Shklovsky would say.

Humour also humanizes. Something you can joke about seems less terrible, but also someone you can joke about seems less frightening or perhaps different.

You know those red security locks that lock onto the steering wheel of your car – the Club – to protect it from thieves? My wife, who is a criminal lawyer, had a client who stole a car fitted with one. The police chased him. Thing is, with the Club, the guy was only able to turn the steering wheel in one direction. And Hamilton is a city of one-way streets. So the police are chasing him, and all he can do is turn left and left and left again as he tries to make his getaway, but he can just spiral inward until finally, of course, the police catch up and arrest him.

Perhaps we can see some aspect of ourselves in this hapless car thief. We can relate somehow. We recognize ourselves or someone we know in that story. At the very least, the thief doesn't seem threatening or scary.

Here's one of my favourite poems. It's by an English professor, Martin Laba. It's called "Modern Poem," and it goes like this:

one, two,

three, four,

five, you idiot.

I like it because we can empathize with the feeling of having read something, perhaps a modern poem, something that is so hard to understand, that appears to be saying something willfully inaccessible or that appears so entirely pointless that it seems to be deliberately trying to make you feel like an idiot. I like the poem because of the nice twist, the surprise at the end, the shock of recognition. Oh yes, I know poems like this. And I know that feeling.

Another aspect of humour is the you-can't-fire-me-I-quit principle. When I make fun of myself, when I laugh at myself and my people, when I'm being self-deprecating, there's nothing you can say, because I got there first and have already defined myself.

My father used to be president of Planned Parenthood. I asked him once, when is a Jewish fetus considered viable? He told me it was when it graduated from either law or medical school.

Once, when my kids were little, we were celebrating Passover. There are a number of foods that are traditional to have on the table. Each of them is symbolic of the Passover story, which is about when the Jews were slaves in Egypt. And as the narrator of my novel says, you know what they say about being a slave … at least you have job security. But to return to the Passover Seder, there is salt water, which represents the tears of the enslaved Jews. There's a kind of nut and apple paste, which represents the mortar the slaves used to build the pyramids. And there are two kinds of bitter herbs, used to represent the bitter life of the slaves. My kids asked me, "Why are there two kinds of bitter herbs, what does the second one represent?" We looked it up. Why are there two kinds of bitter herbs? According to some old wise rabbis, the second bitter herbs are there so that children will ask questions. I love this answer. It is, of course, a kind of joke, but it also points to something that, at their best, both Judaism and humour do. They cause you to ask questions. They value surprise and new ways of looking at things. Like the scientific method, they both ask: What if? And why?

In *Yiddish for Pirates*, I have my pirate and his parrot speak Yiddish. Why? Because of its inherent humour and its vitality, its ability to sum up the richness of experience and Jewish being in the world. Wherever Jews went, with or without possessions, they also brought their language. And for me, Yiddish expresses a quintessentially Jewish irony and a fatalistic yet celebratory humour. They tried to kill us but instead we lived and created a new holiday that we celebrate with good food and family. Life is hard, but still, we're around and can tell jokes about it. My novel highlights this kind of humour amid the darkness, a tool we can use in the face of abject adversity. Jews are often a pessimistically optimistic people. Is the glass half full or half empty? Full-shmull. As long as we have a glass.

In my novel, I adapted a few anecdotes from the memoir of a family friend, Erwyn Koranyi, who survived the Holocaust. One amazing story tells of how this Jewish guy named Dolly Heisler escaped the Nazis. Dolly said that the difference between someone who is a prisoner and someone who is not is that the prisoner looks unshaven and dishevelled, and so he always kept razor blades in the lapels of his jacket, just in case he was picked up by the Nazis. One day, he was arrested. He was held for a while, but he had his trusty razor blades in his lapels, and so he was able to keep himself clean-shaven and fresh-faced. He heard a Nazi asking for an interpreter, and so he stepped up and said, "I'm the translator.

I can't wait to help do something about these stinking Jews." He spent the day translating and then, when a driver appeared, he asked casually if after work he could get a ride downtown. The driver said, "Well, I can't give you a ride, but my boss, Eichmann, is going downtown." And so, this guy, Dolly Heisler, escaped imprisonment by the Nazis by getting a ride with Adolf Eichmann.

There's an empowering daring in this story, an escape that is resourceful, courageous and has a kind of insouciant bravura to it. But it's also funny. The surprise of it. The delightful empowering chutzpah of the guy.

*

Finally, humour is about the pleasure of storytelling. The plot twists and delicious surprises. The opportunity to amuse and delight, to draw the reader in and lead them down the dramatic garden path. It enables the writer to confront difficult material, to give the reader a way in and, perhaps while entertaining them, render them open to a sneak attack of emotion or meaning. As Victor Coleman wrote of the work of Stuart Ross, "the message in the chuckle is a punch in the gut."

What's the difference between tragedy and comedy? I did some research. Mel Brooks says that "Tragedy is when I cut my finger, comedy is when you walk into an open sewer and die."

There it is. The delicious surprise of the take-no-prisoners ending. Which reminds me. There was this sailor, Yankeleh.

He leaves a pair of pants to be repaired baym shnayder – at the tailor. After seven years, now covered in scars and tattoos, he returns to pick up his pants. They aren't ready.

"Gevalt!" Yankeleh exclaims. "It only took Adonai himself six days to make the world. You've had six years!"

"What's to say, now that the world is done?" the tailor replies. "So, nu, your pants are a tragedy … but at least we can talk about them."

*

And that's the point. We can talk together. About pants. About the world. About our lives. We tell our stories and the stories of those we know. We tell stories about the way the world is and the way the world could be. Sometimes we tell easy stories, sometimes difficult stories. But always with compassion, intelligence, wit and humour.

To quote Aaron, my parrot narrator: "Ach, it's a life. A wonder tale. And we try not to notice that – can we help it? – all the time our tucheses are plonked in the sitz-bath of 'story.' You think, genugshoyn, enough already. But nu. Gey plotz. What can you do? You try not to let tsuris – your troubles – make you old."

Which reminds me:

A man goes to the theatre with his son.

"One adult and one child," he says at the box office.

"That's no child," the ticket seller says. "He looks at least thirty."

"I can help it that he worries?"

Often we tell our most important or our least important stories with humour. As I said, I believe that humour is one of the great technologies, one of the great tools of humankind. For investigation. For community. For keeping on keeping on. Our stories tell us that we're in this together, and together we tell our stories from beginning to our end.

So tell me, Moishe, your parrot – alev ha-shalom – may he rest in peace, such a good imitator he was, what were his last words?

My parrot's last words? What were my parrot's last words? They were: "Oy gevalt! I think my parrot is having a heart attack?"

LANGUAGE AND A HALF

[...]

They write – the world is made of tiny particles. Waves. Strings. Various forces which are things and things which are forces, secret wires that make the visible, entangled and strange. And another kind of tangle: ideas that are signs and signs that are ideas.

In Jewish thought, the letters of the alefbeit predated the creation of the world. In fact, the world was *made* out of these letters, these strange scrapings on the brainscape of the infinite. And each Hebrew letter is a story, a symbolic arrangement of its parts. This little hadron went to market, and this one tore the previous universe a new one.

Inside the brain, there's the shape of a little person. The homunculus of one's greater self. The shape of hands, face, one's mother and father, night, thunderstorm. The shape of each letter. The homunculus is a kind of letter. A sigil inside the head. The brain doesn't only contain a representation of the script (and the script) of one's conceptual story, the brain *is* these things. It is made of them. Its convolutions and thickets take the form of what they represent. Language does this. [...]

But whose language? How can we [re]write [re]writing, ensure we're not snared, entangled. Uh, power structures, epistemological colonization. Yeah, capitalism (I'm not just talking the beginning of proper nouns) and ideology. [...] Don't take me for an ideogram. A hippograph.

But back to basics. An *A. A W.* An ampersand. The Hebrew letter shin (ש). Ellipses, those no-see-um markers that represent what isn't there. [...] If one wants to edit out the ellipses, one needs to put them back in, in order to signal that they are gone.

A door is a door, but it is also the Hebrew letter dalet (ד). Why am

I telling you this? I don't even speak or write Hebrew. But that's why. As a child, I sat in synagogue and marvelled at books filled with knurls that were letters. Scrolls filled with them, lung-sized rectangles of close-inked text on sewn-together pages of parchment; letters, crowned exoskeletons both etymological and entomological. Scrolls crowned in literal silver crowns, wrapped in velvet, kept in a gold-lit ark. [...] The sounds of chanting, the cantor with a silver pointer in the shape of a pointing finger. And the marvel that these letterforms, these mouth shapes, were unintelligible to me except as script or music. The calligraphic maze. An amazement. The shapes of letters as tactile, aesthetic, their meaning not in their meaning but in their form, the inky music of looking, the region of the brain, evolving with these letters, the calligraphic region, the frontal majuscule, cerebral longhand, the amygdalet (ד), the homunculus not holding a pen but made of language, of letters. [...]

Language is pataphysical. Alfred Jarry's term for an imaginary solution to a real problem. The real distillation of imagined reality.

Here's a parenthesis.) Here's another. (. Together)(. What lies outside except everything. All language. The set of everything that can be written. And that which cannot. Now what is outside of the spoken. " ... "

Oh, that's a language. That's a language-and-a-half.

Wittgenstein says, "What we cannot speak about we must pass over in silence." But that's where it gets interesting. It's where we learn about speaking, about language. [...] What if we speak about what we cannot speak? If we write what we cannot write? If we remain where we let ourselves almost fall but catch ourselves. If we see how far language will take us. If we're taken in, or out. Language, the a priori trickster. If [...] had wanted a connection between reality and language, [...]'d have made reality out of language, and given us the world to communicate with.

[...]

HITLER'S MOUSTACHE, MY GRANDFATHER'S LIP

In the hallway just outside the preschool, pictures of past synagogue presidents. First names: Jacob, Jacob, Louis, Max, Adolph, Jacob, Adolf, Max, Moses, Adolph, Samuel, Sam, Aaron, Joe, Joseph, Moses, Leo, Adam. At a certain point, the name Adolf falls out of fashion.

At another point, Hitler's moustache and my grandfather's traded places. Did they pass in the street and one jumped off the upper lip of the other? Did the Führer sneeze during a salute and my grandfather, hiding in an alley, sneeze at the exact same time, and so the trade was made? Such mysteries can never be known. Eventually, my grandfather and the new moustache emigrated to South Africa. My grandfather's original moustache hid beneath Berlin, on Hitler's lip, then was blown away with the rest of Hitler's face as the Allies entered the city and Hitler shot Eva Braun and then himself.

The idea that a growth of hair could have a name is strange but also telling. Vandyke, Fu Manchu, Charlie Chaplin. Did my grandfather initially adopt the look because he was emulating the Little Tramp, Oliver Hardy, a truncated Groucho Marx? Pratfalling his way out of history, somehow escaping what he knew was soon to occur?

The Nazi moustache on my grandfather's lip made calls on the wall phone late at night, when my grandfather would sleepwalk into the kitchen. Germany. France. Argentina. Brazil. Can a moustache cry? A moustache can cry. It can also move money from one offshore account to another. It spoke to beards. To pointed sheets. To shoes whose shine reflected a vast network of stars and small planes that flew overhead. Sometimes it would sing sweet German songs.

Mein Liebchen, wir sassen beisammen
Traulich im leichten Kahn;

My sweet one, we sat together,
We loved one other in our light boat.

My grandfather's original moustache woke up several years after Berlin was divided between east and west. It barely remembered what had happened. It would play chess in the park. It got foam from Viennese coffee on its hairs. It read newspapers in the library. It spoke to émigrés.

The name Adolf appeared more in 1937 than at any other time. It was used infrequently until about 1920. After 1937 there was a steep decline, another small peak in 1964 (the year I was born) and then a gentler decrease, although its use has continued to rise until the present day.

According to Wikipedia, my grandfather's "toothbrush" style of moustache first became popular in the United States in the late nineteenth century; from there it spread to Germany and elsewhere, reaching a height of popularity in the interwar years, before becoming unfashionable after World War II due to its strong association with Hitler. The association is strong enough now that the toothbrush has become known as the "Hitler moustache."

One story attributes gas masks as the reason Hitler trimmed his more fulsome Kaiser-style moustache. As a soldier in the First World War, his mask did not seal and so he had to trim his facial hair until it achieved its iconic shape. Another attributes a stay in Liverpool, the "lost years" of 1917 and 1918, with his sister-in-law Bridget. Apparently, they argued over many things including his unkempt facial hair, and so she cut it.

The preschool in the synagogue is in Temple Anshe Sholom, the oldest Reform Synagogue in Canada, founded in the early 1850s by a small group of German Jewish families who settled in the city of Hamilton. My children attended this school in the 1990s. It was run by a woman called Celia Berlin, and so I called the protective divider between the hall and the school the Berlin Wall.

I remember standing on a gentle hill in Ireland, in soft light with my father. A small white car drove by. A VW. My father said his father would never buy one because it was German. When I was a teenager, my father bought a Mercedes. It was a beautiful and well-made car. The doors closed with a precise click. "To keep in the Zyklon-B," I said.

Hitler's moustache eventually immigrated to Canada with my grandparents. First to Moncton, New Brunswick, then to Vancouver and finally, when my grandfather was ill, to Ottawa to be with my doctor father. I remember hearing my grandparents coughing when they woke in the morning. Both had been heavy smokers. And no wonder, my grandfather owned a tobacconist's shop for many years. My grandfather sitting on a bench by an outdoor hockey rink, Hitler's moustache fluttering slightly in the cold breeze. My brother skating. Then my grandfather and the moustache listening to me play Bach on alto saxophone in our kitchen. My grandfather's watery patient eyes. Did the moustache make late-night calls from Ottawa? Did it attempt to gain support for taking over new countries, or for the rebirth of the will? It seemed meek, listening to the Bach sarabande and the bourrée, the gavotte and the gigue. Then my performance of Mancini's "The Pink Panther Theme."

Once I was in my bed reading *The Count of Monte Cristo* when my grandfather's moustache came into the room. I recognized it as it stood in the dim light near the door, even though it had not been on my grandfather's lip since before I had been born. Before even my father had been born, before my grandfather escaped to South Africa. "Does the other moustache know you are here?" I asked. It had travelled from

Berlin and somehow found me, my grandfather and Hitler's moustache. "Shh," it said. "I don't want them to hear." Then it began to quietly sing the Sh'ma, the central prayer of Jewish identity.

In the Warsaw Ghetto, the Nazis tried to hold a roll call to determine who to send to the death camps. The guards insisted the Jews count faster and faster until finally, as an act of resistance, they sang the Sh'ma. Schoenberg's *A Survivor from Warsaw* tells the story, beginning with, "I cannot remember everything. I must have been unconscious most of the time."

There is a long tradition of magic in Jewish tradition. One scholar notes that, still, many modern Jews employ practices that are quite like protective charms. Observant Jews wear tefillin for morning prayer – small boxes held to the upper arm and forehead by leather straps. Prayer scrolls in a special case mounted on doorframes. Both contain prayers, including the Sh'ma.

As soon as I was old enough, in fact before, I grew a beard and a moustache. Both were protective charms. Magic to protect me. From fear. Time. Society. Not growing.

Wikipedia again:

During puberty, the first facial hair to appear tends to grow at the corners of the upper lip (age 11–15) then spreads to form a moustache over the entire upper lip (age 16–17).

This is followed by the appearance of hair on the upper part of the cheeks and the area under the lower lip (age 16–18) which eventually spreads to the sides and lower border of the chin and the rest of the lower face to form a full beard (age 17–21).

The moustache showed me stars out the window. Constellations that appeared in northern skies. Then we planned how it might return to my grandfather's lip, how we might vanquish Hitler's moustache. Not with a razor or clippers but with cunning and careful planning. How should the moustache feel? What should we say? Who should we consult?

Nazis who wore Hitler moustaches include Karl Maria Demelhuber, Sepp Dietrich, Irmfried Eberl, August Eigruber, Hermann Esser, Julius Streicher, Franz Ritter von Epp, Christian Wirth and Kurt Zeitzler. Many others have worn the moustache including Fred Trump, prominent Israeli politicians and Robert Mugabe.

My granny and grandpa's bed sat against the window. My grandfather wore an eye mask to keep out the beams of the streetlights. In sleep, my grandmother looked like a child, worried yet earnest. Years later, when she was dying of cancer, I sat by her bed to say what I expected would be my last words to her. Because of her illness, she had been unresponsive, seemingly unable to understand or communicate. "I love you," I said, though I was embarrassed. She smiled as if she understood.

The moustache and I crept to my grandfather's side of the bed. There it was, Hitler's moustache. Even in the half-light, I could see what I had not been able to. There was something not right about the moustache on my grandfather. "Should we wake him? Should we tell him?" "Let him sleep," the moustache said. I followed its instructions. We each had our jobs. The moustache would leap onto my grandfather's lip after I'd finished.

I slowly lowered my fingers over my grandfather's face and then took firm hold of the moustache and pulled quickly, as if removing a Band-Aid. Then I ran, the moustache in my hand. I ran down the stairs, out the front door and into the street. I ran toward the park, gripped a rock and, putting the moustache on the end of a slide, pounded. Pounded. The metal of the slide clanged loud in the night, a muted bell. I pounded the moustache with the rock again and again. Again and again. The moustache had been flat but become even flatter. Did I sing the Sh'ma Yisrael? I said nothing.

RACING FUTURITY

We had just buried a relative of my wife's. Because the grave was near my grandfather's, the same grandfather our four-year-old son was named after, we went to show him the grave and to pay our respects. Our son, seeing his name on the stone and knowing he could get a rise out of us, if not his late great-grandfather, lay down on the grave and crossed his hands as if flying into himself (as Bill Knott's poem puts it). As if dead at four years old, our little son stretched out in front of a gravestone with his name on it. Of course he got a rise out of us.

*

I've never visited the grave of someone I love. Loved. Except if I happen to be in the cemetery for a funeral or an unveiling.

Unveiling: the Jewish custom of waiting a year – or in these modern times, less than a year – to place a stone on the grave and "unveil" it, marking the end of the official year of mourning.

*

I don't know where my grandfather "is." He's now not a human being but a human was-ing. Whatever the great mystery of life and death, his body is certainly not alive and, all these years later, is likely not much more than bones. What's Yeats' line about an old man being "a tattered coat upon a stick"? Forty years after his death, if my grandfather's body is anything, it's all stick, not coat. Strange then, to "pay our respects" in this particular place.

I know the funeral plot is really just a placeholder, a focal point for our memories. Easier than looking everywhere and nowhere. Like the bomb victim whose stone said, "Rest in Pieces."

*

There is a grave my kids and I used to visit in the Royal Botanical Gardens in Hamilton. Hidden in a "small grove north of the Scented Garden in

Hendrie Park,"[1] the headstone says: Martimas. A good horse. And a sire of good horses.

That's me. A good horse. And a sire of good horses. I want to be a good father.

*

Martimas was a racehorse, "foaled 1896 – died 1916," owned by William Hendrie who owned the land where the horse was buried. Hendrie raised draft horses for his cartage business as well as racehorses for, well, races. He was proud of Martimas's accomplishments and so he erected this large headstone.

Apparently, it's not clear if all of Martimas is buried beneath the headstone or just his head. Why separate the head from the body? Is this a mind-body thing? Did the jockey want a souvenir? Was it a forerunner of *The Godfather*, the horse's head in someone's bed?

*

A rhyme I'd recite for my kids when they were young:

1-1 was a racehorse
1-2 was 1 2
1-1 1 1 race
and 1-2 1 1 2.

*

It's traditional for Jews to recite "The Mourner's Kaddish" each morning in synagogue for a year after a parent dies. Yit-ga-dal v'yit-ka-dash sh'mei ra-ba. One should say this Aramaic prayer with other people. A minyan. Traditionally (because, you know, misogyny) a group of ten men. Sometimes people ask, "Who will say kaddish for me?" I know my father-in-law has wondered this, and I think it might end up being me. I live closest to the synagogue. It's not something I believe in, but it is something I'd do in some form and for some length of time because it was important to him.

John Cage said, "If something is boring after two minutes, try it for four. If still boring, then eight, sixteen, thirty-two, and so on. Eventually one discovers that it's not boring at all."[2] I think it's also true that you learn something from doing almost anything many times. Just by waking up early, going to the synagogue, reciting the same Aramaic prayer, surely something will be revealed. I think it'd be relational, and I'm not talking God. All that time in a particular place with others, there for a variety of complex reasons themselves. And performing this ritual for someone else I'd expect a wide range of feelings: sorrow, frustration, resentment, boredom, love, bewilderment. A sense of understanding, realization or unreality; of connection or disconnection with the tradition of my ancestors.

*

In 1898, Martimas won the race for the best two-year-old horse in America, the Futurity Prize. William Hendrie used the prize money to pay for a wing of Hamilton General Hospital to be built in Martimas's name. Strange to be treated in a part of a hospital named for a horse. Since he won some significant races, and sired some significant racing horses and thus left a significant legacy, Martimas (both his head and his body) was eventually given a place in the Canadian Horse Racing Hall of Fame.

*

There's a headstone near where my wife's grandparents are buried. The inscription doesn't say the usual – "beloved husband and father, much missed grandfather" – but something to the effect of, the guy came second in the city chess championships, first in checkers. I always thought it was quite sad, that this was what he wanted written on "his final resting place." And he wasn't even first in chess. But when

I mentioned it to my son, he made the good point that I really didn't know anything about the guy and I was being "judgy."

What would I want on my stone, what would I want to be remembered by? I don't think I'd rely on an inscription on a headstone for that. Or even to be in one place. I'd rather be spread out like that joke about the bomb victim, resting in pieces. Bits of me everywhere – in lakes, forests, fields. Those who knew me would remember me in their own ways. As husband, father, maybe one day grandfather. As friend, colleague, co-conspirator.

*

In his poem "After Thomas Hardy's 'Afterwards,'" David W. McFadden, always a trickster, upending our expectations and solemn certainties, our glib platitudes, reflects on how he might be remembered.

> After I'm dead/ ...
> a child will pick up
> a piece of dog shit
> & taste it
>
> & someone will say Look!
> McFadden was a man who
> would have noticed that.

*

I don't imagine what it might be like after I'm dead. For me or for others. Maybe my family and the people who knew me might look at things in the world and be aware of how I might have thought of them. "Look!" He "would have noticed that." Maybe my children will think about our times walking through forests, on the shores of lakes, among shopping carts in parking lots. I don't think they'll remember what I said but more how I might have said it, or the kinds of things I might have been apt to say or think. What I might have radiated in their presence about being in the world. And concerning our relationship. It's not so much who I was but how I was with them. Or maybe who I hoped to be.

*

I resist the notion of thinking of a posthumous summing up of one's life, the Coles Notes of who you were. The Yelp review, the Goodreads commentary. There was some humour in the life. There were some animals in the life, but toward the end, I got lost. I did not understand any of it. To me this life was quite good in the beginning and middle. End ... lost me totally. Two stars.

Certainly others might do a summing up of your life after you're gone, but I don't believe in thinking about it prehumously or of living for how you might be remembered, other than trying to not be the kind of person people are glad to see the coffin lid of, or must speak about in psychotherapy.

Likely, I'll end up in a patch of ground somewhere, though I'd prefer not, but laws being what they are, and also because my wife would like us to be in a discreet place. And by discreet I don't mean out of public view as we'll be spending eternity making the xylophone with two backs with our naked bones. I mean in a single identifiable place. My wife wants us to be buried together, embracing for eternity, a cat's cradle of bones. And of course, I want our eternity to be together – however time and space might turn out. Like that passage of strange and loving beauty by John Berger: "What reconciles me to my own death more than anything else is the image of a place: a place where your bones and mine are buried, thrown, uncovered, together ... With you I can imagine a place where to be phosphate of calcium is enough."

All very lovely, but it does lead me to wonder if the plan is to die together. Or, after one or other of us dies, the grave is opened and, according to a precise IKEA-like assembly plan, our bones are fitted together into this final and eternal embrace, and then the lid of earth put back on like a patch of hair after neurosurgery.

*

Do I think about the living archive of my now adult children, how they embody my bodiless legacy in more ways than just being a sack half-filled with my DNA? That something of the way they live and who they are is because of me? Though somewhat true, I don't consider this, except perhaps when they're feeling badly and I wish I had better prepared them for adversity. Or given them supercharged "very satisfied with life" genes. Otherwise, their qualities are their own, even if I can identify some aspects that perhaps connect to me. I might have given them the violin, but they learned to play it – violin here as both an expression of values as well as a physical inheritance. Nature. Nurture. Stradivari.

*

In breeding horses, breeders consider personality as well as the physical. Certainly, Martimas's progeny – Kelvin, Shimonese and Slipper Day – were race-winning animals, a fact attributable to both mind and body. In 1911, the *Daily Racing Form* wrote that Slipper Day, owned by Hendrie's son, John, who became the eleventh lieutenant-governor of Ontario, was "the fastest filly ever bred in Canada."

*

Incidentally Martimas's sire was Candlemas, his dam Biggonet; the "mas" suffix in Martimas inherited from his sire. I've often wondered about the tradition of naming your children after you. Or with names that refer to you. John and John Jr. Or Johann Sebastian, Johann Friedrich, Johann Christoph. In Iceland, surnames are built from the father's name. Björk is Björk Guðmundsdóttir, which is Björk, the daughter of Guðmundur. In traditional Jewish naming, it works the same way. In synagogue, I'm Gershon Ben Nachmann (and now v'Miriam). Gary son of Norman (and Myrna). I think it'd have been years (more) of therapy if I'd named my kids after me, though. In Ashkenazi Jewish tradition, it is very bad luck to name a baby after a living person, but the proper thing to do is to name them after a dead relative. Hence my son was named after his great-grandfather. I do like the idea of continuity. Not that there are qualities that my son shares with his great-grandfather, just that he's connected with his ancestors, if only by this custom.

*

There's a Jewish tradition that rather than leaving flowers at a grave, you place a stone on the gravestone. That's some imitative magic there. Stone on stone. There is something elemental and solemn about using a stone. Nothing says gravitas like stone. And the stone stands in for earth or ground. Where the loved one is. And time is as long and enduring as stone. And as long as the remembrance of the dead. And more enduring than flowers, those fussy, bright living-but-not-for-too-long things.

Another idea is that the stone keeps the soul in the world. Hey, you want to go to paradise? Sorry, Charlie, I'm plunking a rock on top of your grave to hold you down. Another idea is that it stops golems and demons from getting in. Think I'll go bring evil to this dead soul. Oh no. There a small rock in the way. Guess I'll go to Washington instead.

Of course – because Judaism – there's also a language reason. Apparently, the Hebrew word for "pebble" – tz'ror – is the same as the word for "bond." According to the Star of David Memorial Chapels' website, "When we pray ... we ask that the deceased be 'bound up in the bond of life' – tz'ror haHayyim. By placing the stone, we show that we have been there, and that the individual's memory continues to live on in and through us."[3] My word for pebble is my bond.

*

I have placed stones on gravestones. I've also lifted stones, cupped them in my hands, felt their heft, that they are made of the earth as well as archetype. Something bigger. Whenever I lift a stone I think of history, of those who have died, perhaps buried beneath headstones. Of those who have been lost. Sorrow turned to stone? A petrified ritual? Charles Simic evokes the mystery of a stone in his famous and mysteriously named poem "Stone":

> I have seen sparks fly out
> When two stones are rubbed,
>
> . . . .
>
> Just enough light to make out
> The strange writings, the star-charts
> On the inner walls.

When I lift a stone, I think of those who have no headstone, those who are buried beneath stones in unmarked earth. The parents of that great-grandfather after whom we named our son, my great-grand-parents, were shot in a small town outside of the city of Panevėžys, Lithuania, during the Holocaust. Through archival research, I found details of their death in a registry. The name of the town. The approximate date. My grandfather was told about their murder years later by a drunk guest at a Bar Mitzvah in South Africa. He came home and told my teenage father. Simic:

> Let somebody else become a dove
> Or gnash with a tiger's tooth.
> I am happy to be a stone.

*

In the end, it's not entirely up to me how I am remembered. I'd be gratified if people kept reading – or began to read – my writing and listened to my music. I'd be touched if some thought, "He strove that such innocent creatures should come to no harm," or even "He was one who had an eye for such mysteries."[4] But it's more about this life, while I am alive, trying my best to be a good horse. Not to be remembered as a sire of good horses, though my children are that, but as a good sire. Friend. Husband. Person. I don't expect any of us to win a horse race.

LETTER TO YOU AS IF YOU WERE KAFKA

In this letter, I'm going to pretend you are Kafka. Nocturnal. Secretive. Intense.

Pained yet quietly open to the joy in the world.

And tonight, I saw – or didn't see – something which reminded me of you. After midnight, as I walked the dog, I saw a figure on the path. The forest was blue and bright because of the full moon; even the shadows were blue. The dog howled and began to run, but I called him back. I couldn't tell if the figure was coming toward us or heading away. We kept walking and the figure appeared to stride off into the trees. Maybe it was a trick of the turning path, but when we rounded the bend, it was gone. The dog nosed disconsolately for a minute then gave up. It was unsettling, alone at night in the woods and this figure appearing seemingly out of nowhere. What was it?

As I'm writing this, I feel as if I'm missing out on the other writing I could be doing.

Remember that summer we watched the waves fall onto the shore, the tide coming in, the waves coming closer and closer, so near to the sandcastles we'd made? Eventually you couldn't stand it and so ran up to them and smashed them all.

Kafka wrote a famous letter to his father, filled with bitterness and recrimination. He never sent it, but it's become posthumously famous since Max Brod saved his friend's writing from his wished-for fire. But I like best Kafka's letters to his partners, such as Milena. There's often an intimate joy and the sense of loving attention, to the world and to Milena.

I'm living quite well here, the mortal body could hardly stand more care, the balcony outside my room is sunk into a garden, overgrown and covered with blooming bushes (the vegetation here is strange; in weather cold enough to make the puddles freeze in Prague, blossoms are slowly unfolding before my balcony), moreover this garden receives full sun (or full cloud, as it has for almost a week). – lizards and birds, unlikely couples, come visit me: I would very much like to share Meran with you, recently you wrote about not being able to breathe, that image and its meaning are very close to one another and here both would find a little relief.[1]

That's how I would like this letter to feel. Dispensing with protective or habitual distance, if we could speak earnestly and straightforwardly, even if we don't agree. If it could be based on listening, really seeing each other, and authentic connection. I think so much pain and confusion could be alleviated if we only had the feeling of being seen.

After returning from the walk, I lay down and dreamt that all of the ink from all the world's writing was distilled into a vast tank, like liquid night. Then someone was dropped in and their body stained blue as they struggled to breathe. They pressed against the glass as if a desperate sea creature. Later, there was a war and the tank was tipped over, ink flooding into the fields and streets. All those words – serifs, ascenders, bowls – released into the world.

*

Yesterday, Zoe Whittall posted on TwiXter that a friend had reminded her that "gay bars used to end the night with three slow songs so we'd go off into the night after swaying around holding each other and I think we should bring back that tradition."

I responded, "I think all gatherings, meetings, grocery shopping trips should end this way."

I used to be invested in irony and was quite cynical, though I might have said something about engaging in the absurdity and contingency of everything. I'd shy away from direct expression (where is the complicating nuance?) and anything that could smack even slightly of sentimentality. But now I feel like saying, "Fuck that shit." My friend and collaborator Lillian Nećakov and I were discussing why we and many of our peers are writing about death and have an interest in "deeper thinking." Is it the times or our age – sixty or more?

I believe the hands of the clock are too close to midnight, and anyway, this kind of post-ironic honesty is a response to how capitalism erodes our values and sense of self. I'm trying to think without the carapace, to speak from the squishy, un-deflecting, unguarded self, hoping that I'm able to withstand whatever the consequences are. I both feel that I've been around long enough to be strong enough for it and that I've learned from many brave souls, speaking from many places of alterity – queer, disabled, BIPOC – telling what is true for them.

*

A wolf in front of me. I wait. A forest grows. A wolf and me and the trees. I wait more. The wolf is bones. I will not be late to the chess game.

*

Do I believe that words are enough? Words spoken to you or words written, would they change things, be helpful? Change is more of a process, I believe. The formation of a new pattern. How many days does it take to form a habit? Answer (backed by science!): sixty-six days.[2] (I'm beginning to feel like I'm channelling the second-personing of the letter-writing Rilke.)

Perhaps a thought finds its way into your thinking and, like a computer virus, begins to replicate, working in the background, making changes that may at first be invisible. The thin edge of a wedge doesn't break the rock, but after some time and some worming, more of the wedge wedges between the rock-flesh and splits it (so it "bursts like a star," to quote

Rilke). A single statement may have echoes. And perhaps the attention, the care, the seeing is the first thing that makes a difference, that allows the exchange to take root. A letter is read, maybe only partially, then put down. But then picked up again, either literally or in the mind.

*

In his "Archaic Torso of Apollo," Rilke exhorts, "You must change your life." Err, okay. I'd never thought of that. I'll change it, right away. Thanks, Rainer. Of course, we wonder "change how?" And rather than just following instructions, the phrase becomes more active because we consider what it means. If it even is – like I'm doing here – possible to be told to change, as if thinking something can make a more fundamental change possible. But at least for this letter, what comes before this iconic and often motivationally memed line is important. Translations vary, but the point is:

> for there is no angle from which
> it cannot see you. You have to change your life.[3]

or

> for here there is no place
> that does not see you. You must change your life.[4]

The torso of Apollo sees you wherever and however you are. Is it a shaming gaze that means you cannot continue to get away with your bullshit? I imagine a judgmental God with an eye like a cue ball, having no pupil. It looks (and judges) in every direction.

I think it means that "you are seen" – that your being and your experience are witnessed. I love that the torso of this famed Greek figure has no head, and so it "sees" in every direction without eyes. It radiates corporeal human life, from one living thing to another. Never mind the cerebral cogitation of rationality, this "being seen" is elemental. It is from this place that the exhortation to "change your life" comes – from a deep, indeed fundamental understanding of the human condition (and this six-pack Greek demigod is definitely conditioned). I'd say from a place of love. An atheist Antinomian grace. You are always already everything.

It is from this place that I'd like to write this letter to you. The real you, not the Franz Kafka we both needed it to be addressed to. I wish it could beam out in every direction, not in words but with a sense that you are seen. You do not need to change your life; you just need to see it. To see below the whitecapped water of its surface and know your innate value. "To call [yourself] beloved, to feel [yourself] / beloved on the earth."[5]

THE SELECTED WALKS

We know now that a walk is not a line of steps releasing a single 'theological' meaning ... but a multi-dimensional space in which a variety of walks, none of them original, blend and clash.

– after Roland Barthes, "The Death of the Author"

There's an intimacy to walking with my dog at night. The dark surrounds us and limits the infinity of space. At night, you can see the shape of the sky as if you were in a vast room, a bell jar bounded by the spangle of stars.

And unlike with the sun, that blazing brazen blaring klieg light, you can have a connection, a one-on-one relationship with the moon. You can look at it. It follows you. It changes shape and colour. Pearl. Silver. Opal. Pus. Semen. Bone. Bloodshot eye, strangely lambent, glowing, translucent. The moon feels personal.

It's often said that poets have an obsession with the moon. "I am convinced," Mary Ruefle writes in *Madness, Rack, and Honey*, "that the first lyric poem was written at night, and that the moon was witness to the event and that the event was witness to the moon."

The moon's mooniness is numinous. Luminescent. It seems to comment, a celestial Greek chorus, an outer space familiar, yet it is all negative capability – even its bright side seems as unknowable as its dark side. And it has a dark side, always in shadow, lonely, facing into the beyond. "Beautiful, beautiful. Magnificent desolation," Buzz Aldrin said as he stepped onto its surface, again according to Mary Ruefle. The moon is the Other, emotional yet silent. Melancholy. We moon around, become loony. It pulls the ocean onto shore, as if it were a blanket and it was time to sleep, to enter the cave of dream, like a ready O, our open mouth an O, our endless ouroboros dreams, lunar, O-shaped or crescent. But the moon reaches not only tides but also those who menstruate who feel its phases or at least share its connection to the month – in poetry, anyway. See? I begin thinking about the moon and get carried away.

We do this a lot, my dog, Happy, and me, out after midnight, driving into the country to walk through fields or closed conservation areas. The other day, I was struck by the absurd beauty of the scene: Happy sticking his head out the car window, me blasting Mozart's *Requiem* as we sped along Highway 5, past the gravel pit, the tractor dealer, the place to buy rocks, the various garden centres and churches. We went for a long walk around the lake as it rained. I put on some Bach.

I thought: Here I am, just another Jew wandering through the rainy woods in Hamilton, Ontario, listening to the *Mass in B minor*, feeling frankly glad to live on planet Earth. I think my mind might explode if I had the additional surprising beauty of another planet to experience.

*

Two nerdy walking moments. A few summers ago, walking in the woods, I broke my big toe on a tree root as I listened on headphones to a lecture by the "Tolkien professor" while wearing Birkenstocks. Though nerdy, perhaps this wasn't as nerdy as when I was as a teenager, and I'd skip down the trail playing tin whistle and imagining I was an elf.

*

A few weeks ago, I was listening to Norwegian folk music and the buzzer on the dryer went off at the exact pitch of the song. Hmm, I thought. That means something. A transcultural time-weaving synchronicity. But it must be that the Sámi shaman knew about Maytag, the boxy white-painted ghost roiling my clothes in its hot yoga Twister insides.

I can't help but relate this conjunction in the world to the entanglement of human relations, that judo of interactions over time. So many points of connection – thoughts, actions, correspondences. A complex ecosystem of feelings, observations, reflections, responses. I'm sitting here in the backyard sun with my dad. He's reading and nodding off, a pleasant afternoon, and so I think of our lifelong entanglement, how we have made so many parts of each other. As has happened with all those I love.

*

My therapist wonders if it's safe for me to walk alone at night. He jokes that, "No, it's okay, Happy, the sheepadoodle, is there to protect you." Maybe the slight possibility of danger is part of it. I'm reminded of that idea in *The Hitchhiker's Guide to the Galaxy* where, since all humanity's problems have been solved, there's a process simulating danger (being chased by wild lions) just to motivate you to do basic things, like getting to the bus. Sometimes walking, I'm entirely relaxed, open to the meander of my thoughts and the night. Sometimes there is a frisson of fear, which sends alertness to the edges of my body. An energizing vigilance. I'm intensely aware of my privilege in this activity, as an average-looking, white, able-bodied man. Also, if I think I hear something, I put on a deep voice and call my dog – with that voice, it's got to be a pit bull – "Rex." Happy knows how to use his privilege and be unthreatening as well. There'd be little I could do, in truth, if I were accosted in this closed conservation area out in the country. Happy's only tool to deal with the unexpected is enthusiasm.

I have seen only one person out here. Someone in the trees, illicitly camping by a fire. I was once assaulted, however, but it was in the mostly closed part of the mall downtown. Two tall teenagers, one of them skateboarding. It was unusual and I thought it was kind of cool, so I watched the guy riding. I wonder if he thought I was judging him – me, a middle-aged white guy looking at a Black kid doing something vaguely forbidden. As he went by, he elbowed me hard and knocked me into the store window of a Victoria's Secret. I remember my face in slow

motion skidding down the fifteen-foot-tall décolletage of a bra model.
I didn't call the security or the police. Hmm, I thought. It's like this.
Complicated. My ribs were bruised for weeks. I was struck by how much
stronger he was than me, that had he chosen to do more, I wouldn't have
been able to resist. Like when my son got jacked as a teenager and would
pick me up and move me around the house just because he could.

Everywhere I go, I have my phone, an ostensible lifeline. Once I
walked through an Icelandic forest (i.e., trees about thirty centimetres
tall) in order to climb an inactive volcano. For two or three hours, I
was aware that I was out in the wide world without phone service, and
that if something happened to me, I wouldn't be able to call for help.
No one knew where I was. I was by myself in the world. Me and the
world, making our own unmediated connection. I had a direct line to
my environment – my signal didn't have to travel into space to bounce
off a satellite.

Walking with a dog is another kind of connection. I'm aware of
what the dog finds interesting – what they look at, smell, chase. And a
man walking alone at night might be creepy or threatening, but a man
walking a dog is a man walking a dog. There's a non-worrisome expla-
nation to his actions. Once I was navigating my way through a blizzard
with my dog, no one else out in the storm. An empty bus drove by,
stopped. The bus driver offered me and my dog a ride in their container
of golden light. Though the absurdity of it appealed to me, the reason
we were out walking was ... to walk. And so I declined. I was a man
walking a dog, and so we kept walking.

*

I often listen to music or audiobooks while I walk, especially at night,
if there aren't any engaging nature sounds – for instance, if I'm wandering neighbourhood streets. There's a particular intimacy to headphones.
Someone is whispering into both your ears – it feels like the sound is

in the centre of your brain, your head turned into an amphitheatre – and you carry this secret conversation around with you, an immersive world. You're under the bell jar of story and sound. The sound leaves memories in the landscape and so I associate certain places with events in the music or story, or a tactile sense of presence mediated through my experience of the sound. "Ah, that thing in that story happened here," I think when I arrive at a particular bend in the road. "This is that story place." Narrative and location, story and geography meet. And then, since I will likely listen to other recordings on the same route, sedimentary layers of stories and music associated with the same place gather. A conjunction of events, some real, some fictional, tangling together, my own idiosyncratic psychogeographic neural network.

*

In post-baroque Western classical music, at a deep level, many works were conceptualized as being narrative, particularly those in sonata form, the emblematic structure of the modern common-practice era. It is a form that reflects the rationalism of the Enlightenment, something of the Hegelian dialectic and also having an aspect of the classical logic of the syllogism about it. The narrative metaphor intensified during the Romantic and late-Romantic era, often made explicit in program music, which explicitly "told" stories, often a quest, a there-and-back-again journey, beginning in the "home" key with defined melodies and then voyaging into new keys, with explorations of melodic and rhythmic ideas, often only fleeting memories of the original material. Then, usually, the music returns home, restating the material in the original ("home") key. It evokes the hero's journey – oh, we've travelled far and returned changed, having learned from the vicissitudes and shifting sands of our adventure. This is very appealing, going out to seek one's fortune, striding into the world and accumulating wisdom (and possibly wealth and power) through adventure.

But that's not how we experience living or walking. We move through time and the ostensible forward direction of our lives, but memory and history accumulate, double back, break expected boundaries like a Möbius strip. A Möbius strip walks into a bar. Bartender: "What's wrong?" Strip: "Where to even begin?"

Of course, no matter where we go, we encounter the world through the frame of our own experience, as if we brought our own soundtrack to every knife fight. Walking while listening allows me to see through, let's say, Bach, for example (or my own experience of Bach). Each note a jeweller's loupe, each melody a window, but the windows are double- or triple-glazed, stained glass with the accumulation of whatever else has been experienced there.

*

It's December and I'm in grade seven playing second alto saxophone in the Intermediate School Band. We're playing "Silver Bells." I can't recall ever having heard the song, but I found the second alto part very moving. We had the harmony to the "Children laughing, people passing" lyric, and I remember a feeling of exquisite tenderness in the downward leap on "laughing," which then repeated on "passing." We humans, how vulnerable we are, but how infinitely touching. I also realized that my part gave me instructions on what to feel, what state to inhabit emotionally. Mezzo forte with a delicate little decrescendo to mezzo piano. My middle school heart was called to experience this intimate human moment as if I were a method actor playing a role. I could merge with all those who felt these big feelings, could be free of my own early teenage tube man of emotions, all that absurd gravitas-less twisting and perennial near deflation. From my second alto chair, I could experience the wide range of what it means to be human, even experience emotions that I understood little about or that were outside the experience of a suburban Ottawa teen. Melancholy, joy, nobility, grief, compassion, insouciance, heroism, happiness, resilience, sexiness, courage. All in simplified band arrangements ranging from the theme to *Hogan's Heroes* to Dvořák's *Slavonic Dances*. And these feelings seemed embodied in the material of the music, the relationship between notes, timbre, dynamics and tempo. By paying attention to what seemed inherent, to the semantic inner life of the music – by listening to what was there in the world, by inhabiting it fully, the walls of the middle school band room fell away and I was in a larger life.

*

I love the syncretic web of experience. Me, in 2023, a Jewish man, born in Northern Ireland and now listening on an iPhone in a conservation area outside Hamilton, Ontario, to a Catholic mass with music composed by a Lutheran in Leipzig in the mid-eighteenth century and presented to the King of Poland and Holy Roman Empire Elector of Saxony. I imagine trying to explain this to one of my medieval ancestors. It reminds me of a poem that I once read where Fred and Wilma Flintstone go to the Grand Canyon and send Barney and Betty a postcard. Fred and Wilma don't think the canyon is a big deal but are mightily impressed by the concept of a postcard.

*

Nineteen seventy-eight. On a tour through Michigan with my high school jazz band, the second trumpeter showed us all this cool new thing he'd bought from a recent trip to New York City: A Sony Walkman. It was a portable audio cassette player with small headphones. I tried it. It astounded me. The sound was entirely inside your head – wherever you walked, you had a soundtrack. This was a revolutionary thing. I'd seen old men – my grandfather included – listen to the news or a ballgame while in the park on a portable radio, sometimes using the single earbud provided. You could hear the broadcast, but it wasn't inside your head. Inside and out were one. With the Walkman, your brain had music right inside it. It was a concert hall. It was a paradigm shift that has become entirely normalized. Everyone has a phone now and most people have earbuds. Audio is portable. We routinely carry around our own soundtrack wherever we go. We don't need to whistle or sing, which is something external (though some still do, often humorously oblivious). The sound is inside us and at the same time surrounds us like the dark.

I went walking with Happy last night. As it was dark and we were in a park, I thought of Charles Ives' *Central Park in the Dark*, a companion piece to his more famous *The Unanswered Question*. Ives' orchestration captures the sound of darkness, the thickness of it, the sense that one is walking through not an absence but a tactile presence. And above the creeping dark of the strings, a mysterious contemplative clarinet and other solo instruments ruminate. (At least until the moment where the unhinged jollity of "Hello! Ma Baby" intrudes, a moment of monkey mind amid introspection.)

My park is Churchill Park, a block away from my home. Because of its proximity to Cootes Paradise and Lake Ontario, the temperature is distinctly colder than the surrounding neighbourhood. The grass is often damp, and deer, having emerged from the adjoining forest, constellate silently in the soccer fields. My last dog, Dude, would sometimes accidently find himself only a metre or so away from a deer and then start in surprise. Happy, on the other hand, spies them from far away and bolts, chasing them as they spring up and dart back into the woods. I've been walking in this park for over thirty years and circling around it, I recall Charles Darwin's path at the back of his property where he would walk round and round while thinking. The routine of the route apparently helped with his thinking. It was something of a ritual, the expectedness and lack of surprise combined with the steady rhythm of walking freed his mind to wander down other paths, to venture down new neural pathways and follow thoughts wherever they might go. I aspire to such satisfying reverie. Sometimes it happens despite the *Hello My Baby* intrusions.

Last night, I considered how solo walking, especially at night, is not like being in a bell jar but like a diving bell. You're carrying your own environment with you yet have a connection to the outside – the air tube. It's ultimately about the self and our connection and individuation from the world. Is it "I am because my little world knows me?" or "I know the world and so I know myself?" Mark Strand:

> In a field
> I am the absence
> of field.
> . . . .
> We all have reasons
> for moving.
> I move
> to keep things whole.

We send out feelers, signals. We echolocate. It's psy(e)chogeography. We sense the shape of our inner landscape by travelling through the one that surrounds us.

Walking with my dog expands this landscape. I think about how he echolocates, what sense of the world and himself he might experience, how we experience each other – a kind of conceptual leash between us, a dog-human umbilical cord. At night, I walk Happy without a leash, so our connection, like Philip Pullman's daemons in *The Golden Compass,* is entirely relational, an invisible attractive force between us. We walk in parallel yet always with one eye on the other.

I quoted Mary Ruefle's line about the creation of the lyric poem, "the moon was witness to the event and ... the event was witness to the moon." That's like my dog and me. The world and me. And walking while wearing headphones, the beginning and end of a Möbius strip made of music, story and imagination. A strange loupe.

There's a Crack in Everything

Three a.m. and we've been pocket-dialled. "Listen," my wife, Beth, says, holding the phone between us. A client of hers is in the middle of burgling a house. "Should we take the TV?" he says to his accomplice. "Nah. Too big. But the computer …" We listened for a while and then hung up. Apparently, they got away with it, as my wife never did get a phone call from the police. Who was the guy? My wife didn't know.

A criminal lawyer, Beth often represents people who have done terrible things, things far more horrifying than breaking into houses. I'm not going to elaborate here because even hearing about these acts casts a shadow and, as a colleague used to say, leaves "dust on your soul."

Beth and I speak of the concept of brokenness: Is anyone "bad" or "evil"? No, we say – we believe, we want to believe – just "broken." There are so many things that can break you. Trauma. Addiction. Physical, sexual and mental abuse. Physical damage before and after birth. Poverty. Mental health. It's a separate issue than what being responsible for one's actions might look like. Certainly, some clients are sent to a psychiatric hospital until such time as it's deemed that they have regained their health. Some are determined not to be "criminally responsible," due to a temporary situation. The law changes as to what causes are pertinent, but, at least in Canada, usually it's not drugs or alcohol.

*

Early crime fiction: Eve eats the apple in Eden then gets expelled. But what about the other apples on the tree? Edmond Jabès writes of a fallen apple rotting on the ground beside the tree. Is that what happens to all the apples on Eve's tree? Do other creatures eat them, or are they infinitely ripe, waiting like the apples in a painting of the scene, timeless as Adam and Eve's needless belly buttons?

What's worse than finding a half a worm in your apple? Finding out the apple comes from the Tree of Good and Evil. Being Eve. Being the worm.

*

When Moses descended Mount Sinai with the tablets, it is said that he lost his temper and smashed them on the mountainside. But he climbed back for seconds, returned with new unbroken tablets, and the Israelites put both broken and whole in the Ark of the Covenant. Maybe the shards of the first tablets were Celan poems, the language not able to contain its own content. But according to the Kabbalah, the world was broken from the beginning, for when God left the world (tzimtzum) he put His divine light in vessels which, not able to contain the light, broke apart and so the light scattered throughout the world. "There's a crack in everything." So now our task is to repair the world (tikkun olam). There go my weekend plans.

*

I was listening to an interview with Sabrina Orah Mark on David Naimon's *Between the Covers* and, in speaking about how her house burnt down, she said it was "beyond surreal, whatever that is." What is beyond surreal? I've been thinking about it. What is not only beyond observable scientifically – verifiable reality – but also what is deeper, more elemental than the reality (the surreality) grounded in our unconscious, or the collective unconscious, the fundamentals of our culture? I thought of different names – xenoreality, parareality, metareality, intersectionalreality – but in addition to not being catchy names, these terms didn't seem to reflect what was more than surreality or capture the multidimensional nature of all reality. Multidimensionality. "Reality" would be better considered not as a continuum – reality then surreality then something beyond that – but as a construct with three or more dimensions.

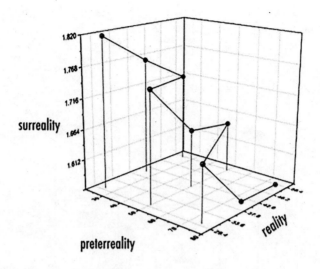

But what would be the dimensions? It occurs to me that there also should be some element of pataphysics, a reality that is constructed through the intercession of human inquiry. The dimension of the imaginary yet necessary.

In the diagram, the line wanders because I imagine that reality isn't a single construct but one that changes through time or perhaps instead depends on the perceiver, narrator or other determinants.

The line looks like a fracture, a fissure, a break. "That's how the light gets in." Perhaps we can fill it in with gold, as in kintsugi ("golden joinery") or kintsukuroi ("golden repair"). Maybe that gold is a kind of light.

But this seems too soft-focus romantic. There's a difference between aestheticizing the brokenness and understanding that there is brokenness – that one must take the broken tablets along with the whole, the imperfect offering, the damaged language and the wounded self. We could instead imagine that the light is our desire to heal, the gold the beauty of repairing – or wanting to repair – the world. We need all the positive feedback we can get.

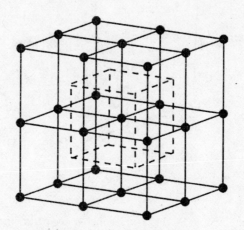

Reality as a 3-dimensional ghost

But back to reality: How are certain things possible in what we think of as reality? The topology of these horrors doesn't fit. After the Holocaust, many couldn't believe that a God could exist that would allow such things. That there could be a reality that could contain such facts. What we knew of the world would have to be changed. Theodor Adorno wrote, "to write poetry after Auschwitz is barbaric," but that would be poetry for the past concept of reality. Poetry and the impulse for poetry would have to exist beyond what was thought of as reality. As if past poetry were for the Newtonian view of the world, the new poetry would have to be Einsteinian. After the "Great War," there were the Dadaists and then the Surrealists. After the Holocaust there was poetry written. The shattered language of Celan, for example.

I've been moved and inspired by Brecht's oft-quoted "Motto":

In the dark times

will there also be singing?

Yes, there will also be singing.

About the dark times.

But there was something about this poem that niggled. I think it's that this "singing" he writes about doesn't speak to the dark times until it is not just "about" them but somehow made from them. Its manner and mode, its structure and physics need also to be dark. The topology of this singing has to occupy all the new dimensions of the darkness.

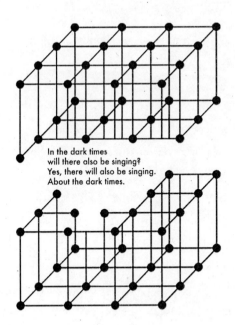

In the dark times
will there also be singing?
Yes, there will also be singing.
About the dark times.

Let's say the sea freezes. A flat, sleek two-dimensional solid. Then someone takes an axe and shatters the surface. (Compare this to Kafka's "a book must be the axe for the frozen sea within us.") Shards of ice splinter, fracture, torque, rise. The endless blue of the dark water visible through the breaks. What was entirely surface is now three-dimensional. I want to relate the plural of axe to the plural of axis, but that seems too neat. Some events are axes.

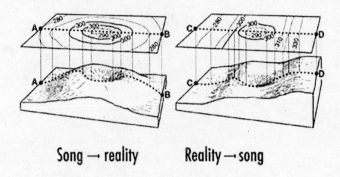

Song → reality   Reality → song

Notwithstanding Adorno's "to write poetry after Auschwitz would be barbaric," we need to attempt to describe and speak to the new reality. Perhaps by repeatedly smashing the tablets in rage, desperation, sorrow.

In "Report from Liberty Street," Charles Bernstein, addressing 9/11, writes that "the question isn't is art up to this but what else is art for?"[1]

*

As Brecht writes, we need songs for the dark times – the original reality, our memory of that reality and the loss of it. But we also need songs for those other realities, the realities which take the shape of the broken sea. And we need the songs for the break, the fracture, the wound.

Since I first encountered them as a teenager, I often think of these lines from Marvin Bell's poem "Gemwood":

Now it seems to me the heart
must enlarge to hold the losses
we have ahead of us.

To me they mean that while we must be ready for what the future brings,
we must also be ready for the extent of the losses of the past and present. Like the universe itself, both past and present never stop expanding.
Heart-rending as it is, reality itself never stops expanding and we encounter its confounding dimensionality. What wasn't possible becomes
possible. What is too much to bear arrives. Also, happiness, joy, escape. Strangeness, beauty, absurdity, the uncertain state of an emotional
Schrödinger box. The basic physics of the world seems to change.

I began thinking about how one could consider "bad" or "evil" behaviour as a form of brokenness. Brokenness bends reality in multiple
dimensions like an imploding star or, actually, anything. Again, I'm not
suggesting that there is no culpability or reckoning with one's actions,
and being a victim is of course a kind of brokenness and also bends
reality, often painfully.

*

Beth had a client who told her, "I used to have a problem with violence,
but now I only hit people when I'm angry with them." And admittedly,
he did deck someone at random on Main St., so this is a significant
improvement. I used to think the line was funny, and it still is in a
way, but now I feel something more akin to compassion. I'm glad he's
been able to identify his feelings – his anger, his pain, his sadness – his
brokenness. This is a substantial development and any healing is impossible without it.

*

I have the impulse to end with something like: we keep on with our box
of broken stone and whatever words we managed to keep intact. And

yes, I think this is true, but this essay should itself be broken, should avoid wrapping things in a bow, even a brokenness-acknowledging bow. Maybe I'll end with an outtake, an image of the Brecht that I tried to make work but didn't.

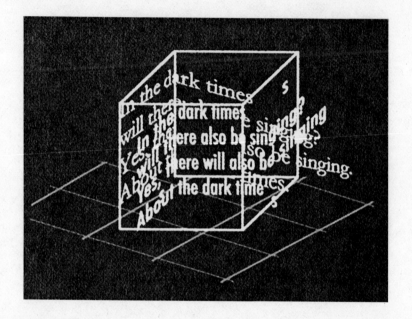

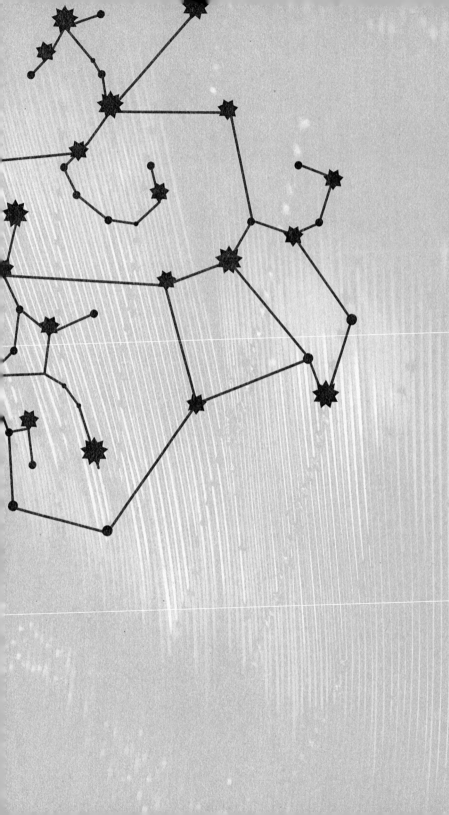

ENDNOTES

Wide Asleep: Night Thoughts on Insomnia

1   "Baruch Spinoza," *Stanford Encyclopedia of Philosophy*, last modified April 16, 2020, https://plato.stanford.edu/entries/spinoza/.

2   It refers to infinite cardinality as opposed to just counting forever, which is ∞.

3   Gwendolyn MacEwen, "Dark Pines Under Water," in *The Shadow-Maker* (Toronto: Macmillan, 1972).

4   Allen Ginsberg, "Howl," in *Selected Poems 1947–1995* (New York: Harper Perennial, 2001).

5   Paraphrased from the traditional version.

6   Paraphrased from Idries Shah, "The Idiot in the Great City," in *Tales of the Dervishes* (Bath, UK: ISF Publishing, 2019), https://idriesshahfoundation.org /books/tales-of-the-dervishes/.

Elegy for a Poodle

1   Mark Strand, "Five Dogs," in *Blizzard of One* (New York: Knopf, 1998).

Three Sides to Everything

1   Michelle, "Vanilla Cream-Filled Doughnuts," Brown Eyed Baker, last updated March 2020, https://www.browneyedbaker.com/vanilla-cream-filled-doughnuts/.

On Between

1   Natalie Diaz, "Natalie Diaz: Postcolonial Love Poem: Part One," interview by David Naimon, *Between the Covers*, audio, https://podcasts.apple.com /us/podcast/natalie-diaz-postcolonial-love-poem-part-one /id583648001?i=1000495735967.

2   David Grimm and Greg Miller, "Is a Dolphin a Person?," *Science*, February 21, 2010, https://www.science.org/content/article/dolphin-person.

3   Sharon Begley, "Brainiacs, Not Birdbrains: Crows Possess Higher Intelligence Long Thought a Primarily Human Tribute," *Stat*, September 24, 2020, https://www.statnews.com/2020/09/24/crows-possess-higher-intelligence -long-thought-primarily-human/.

4   Andreas Nieder, Lysann Wagener and Paul Rinnert, "A Neural Correlate of Sensory Consciousness in a Corvid Bird," *Science 369*, no. 6511 (September 2020): 1626–29, https://www.science.org/doi/10.1126/science.abb1447.

5   Begley, "Brainiacs, Not Birdbrains."

That'll Leave a Mark

1   Walter Benjamin, "The Work of Art in the Age of Mechanical Reproduction," in *Illuminations*, ed. Hannah Arendt, trans. Harry Zohn (New York: Schocken Books, 1969), https://web.mit.edu/allanmc/www/benjamin.pdf.

2   Benjamin, "Work of Art in the Age of Mechanical Reproduction."

The Archive of Theseus

1   Dylan Thomas, "A Few Words of a Kind," lecture, March 7, 1952, Massachusetts Institute of Technology, Cambridge, MA, Soundcloud audio, 9:16, https://soundcloud.com/audio-oddities/dylanth2.

2   Davin Heckman, "'Gotta Catch 'em All': Capitalism, the War Machine, and the Pokémon Trainer," *Rhizomes*, no. 5 (Fall 2002): http://www.rhizomes.net/issue5 /poke/glossary.html.

3   Heckman, "'Gotta Catch 'em All.'" Includes quote from Gilles Deleuze and Felix Guattari, *A Thousand Plateaus: Capitalism and Schizophrenia*, trans. Brian Massumi (Minneapolis: University of Minnesota Press, 1987).

4   Quoted in Heckman, "'Gotta Catch 'em All.'" Includes quote from Deleuze and Guattari.

Sunshine Kvetches of a Little Parrot

1   Adapted from acceptance speech on winning the 2017 Stephen Leacock Memorial Medal for Humour, June 10, 2017, at the Geneva Park Convention Centre, Orillia, Ontario.

Racing Futurity

1   Lauren McAusland, "The Mystery of Martimas, the Horse of Hendrie Park," Royal Botanical Gardens Canada, October 2020, https://www.rbg.ca /the-mystery-of-martimas-the-horse-of-hendrie-park/.

2   John Cage, "Four Statements on the Dance," in *Silence* (Middletown, CT: Wesleyan University Press, 1973), 93.

3   Luisa Luedke, "Why do Jews Place Stones or Pebbles on a Grave?," Star of David Memorial Chapels, Inc., https://www.jewish-funeral-home.com /why-do-jews-place-stones-or-pebbles-on-a-grave/.

4   Thomas Hardy, "Afterwards," in *Moments of Vision and Miscellaneous Verses* (London: Macmillan, 1917).

Letter to You as if You Were Kafka

1   Franz Kafka, *Letters to Milena*, trans. Philip Boehm (New York: Schocken, 2015), https://www.penguinrandomhouse.ca/books/89235 /letters-to-milena-by-franz-kafka/9780805212679/excerpt.

2   James Clear, "How Long Does it Actually Take to Form a New Habit? (Backed by Science)," James Clear, https://jamesclear.com/new-habit.

3   Rainer Maria Rilke, "Torso of an Archaic Apollo," trans. Sarah Stutt, https://writing.upenn.edu/bernstein/syllabi/readings/Rilke-Archaic.html.

4   Rilke, "Torso of an Archaic Apollo," trans. Stephen Mitchell, https://writing. upenn.edu/bernstein/syllabi/readings/Rilke-Archaic.html.

5   Raymond Carver, "Late Fragment," in *A New Path to the Waterfall* (New York: Atlantic Monthly Press, 1994), https://allpoetry.com/late-fragment.

There's a Crack in Everything

1   Charles Bernstein, "Report from Liberty Street," in *All the Whiskey in Heaven* (New York: Farrar, Straus and Giroux, 2011), 263.

ACKNOWLEDGEMENTS

Every time I sit down to write acknowledgements for a book, I don't know where to begin. With gratitude, obviously, but I'm also struck by how my work is part of a vast web of friends, colleagues, acquaintances, writers, thinkers, artists and their work, as well as many other people, experiences and influences. As that old Palmolive ad puts it, "You're soaking in it, Madge." So how to give appropriate thanks. Sure, I could thank the tetrapods for emerging from the sea four hundred million years ago, but that might be overdoing it, plus I'd be leaving out those critically important single-celled organisms, not to mention the Big Bang itself.

I am grateful for the many conversations, both in person and as a reader, that have enabled this book to exist, beginning with Noelle Allen who had the idea for a book of essays in the first place and whose keen editorial advice was invaluable. I'd like to thank the rest of Wolsak & Wynn including brilliant copyeditorr (stet) AGA Wilmot, as well as Ashley Hisson and Jennifer Rawlinson; Kilby Smith-McGregor for another very striking and beautiful design; and Hollay Ghadery, who inventively and enthusiastically helped spread the word.

Most of the essays here were written specifically for the collection, but many were adapted from work written for other occasions, which I've noted below. Thank you to all those involved in the original opportunities. The chance to think and write about these varied subjects and then be able to share it has truly been a privilege.

I've many individuals to thank. My parents, Norman and Myrna Barwin, and my now adult children, Ryan, Rudi and Aaron Bromberg-Barwin. They all enriched this book in innumerable ways, through conversation, sharing knowledge and insights, and through the enlarging and enlivening experience of trying to figure each other out as we navigate our lives.

As should be obvious if you've got to this point in the book, I love to walk and often, whether at night or during the day, I like to listen. Sometimes I listen to the generous, insightful, perspicacious and thoughtful David Naimon and his remarkable podcast, *Between the Covers*. Many of the concerns explored in his conversations found their way in some manner into this book, and so I'm particularly pleased to have his words appear on the back cover. I sincerely appreciate the comments from David and Amanda Leduc, writers whose fiction and non-fiction as well as whose personal integrity I greatly admire.

Musician and writer David Lee contributed important insights, particularly about musical aspects in the writing. I'm also very grateful for the many clarifying and inspiring conversations with writer and collaborator Elee Kraljii Gardiner these last few years. And to Lillian Nećakov for her supportive readings of these essays. It has been a delight to have been able to think about and create public art with Tor Lukasik-Foss and Simon Frank and then to write about it. Further, I'd like to thank Tom Prime, derek beaulieu and Gregory Betts for countless discussions, enthusiasms and creative leads.

Some of the writing appeared in early forms in *Geist*, *The New Quarterly*, *Grain*, *Maclean's*, *Queen's Quarterly*, at Anne Bokma's *6-Minute Memoir*, Jason Camlot's *Shelf Portraits* (the Richler Library Project), through my writer-in-residencies at Sheridan College and Laurier University (the Edna Staebler residency; thanks, Tanis MacDonald), at Magazines Canada (thanks, Hal Niedzviecki), the Leacock Awards, Kathryn Mockler's *Send My Love to Anyone*, the fantastic folks at Ridley College who had a special awards night for creative writers as fancy as the one for athletes, Hamilton Public Library's Power of Pen awards, the openings of my *Broken Light* exhibition at Bryan Prince Bookseller (thanks, Lisa Pijuan-Nomura) and the Beth Jacob Synagogue (thanks, Wendy Schneider). And on the subject of *Broken Light*, Anthony

Etherin and Clara Daneri's Penteract Press (UK) occasioned an early version of the sequence.

I thank the supporters of public funding for the arts through the OAC Writers Reserve grants, which helped with the writing of several of these essays, and more generally for the support that enables the many journals, reading series, publishers and writer residencies, which are also part of this work.

I don't always know how to begin my acknowledgements, but I always know how to end and that is with words of continuous gratitude to my wife, Beth Bromberg-Barwin, who, as I say every time, makes everything possible, but she does. But all right, maybe I'll just name one tetrapod. Thanks, Ichthyostega. Who knew how useful this land thing would turn out be for writers?

Gary Barwin is a writer, composer and multidisciplinary artist. He is the author of thirty books including *Nothing the Same, Everything Haunted: The Ballad of Motl the Cowboy*, which won the Canadian Jewish Literary Award, was shortlisted for the Vine Award and was chosen for Hamilton Reads 2023. His national bestselling novel *Yiddish for Pirates* won the Leacock Medal for Humour and the Canadian Jewish Literary Award, was a finalist for the Governor General's Literary Award for Fiction and the Scotiabank Giller Prize and was long-listed for Canada Reads. His 2022 poetry collection, *The Most Charming Creatures*, won the Canadian Jewish Literary Award. Barwin was born in Northern Ireland of South African parents of Ashkenazi Lithuanian descent. He currently lives in Hamilton, Ontario, and at garybarwin.com.